• Skills for Practice •

Teaching and Learning:
A Guide for Therapists

by

Sally French
BSc, MSc(psych), MSc(soc), Grad Dip Phys, DipTP
Lecturer, School of Health, Welfare and Community
Education, Open University, UK

Susan Neville
MA, MCSP, DipTP
Principal Lecturer,
Department of Rehabilitation Sciences,
University of East London, UK

Jo Laing
BEd
Primary School Teacher, London Borough of Croydon, UK

BUTTERWORTH
HEINEMANN

Butterworth-Heinemann Ltd
Linacre House, Jordan Hill, Oxford OX2 8DP

A member of the Reed Elsevier group

OXFORD   LONDON   BOSTON
MUNICH   NEW DELHI   SINGAPORE   SYDNEY
TOKYO   TORONTO   WELLINGTON

First published 1994

©Butterworth-Heinemann 1994

British Library Cataloguing in Publication Data
A catalogue record for this book is available from the British Library.

ISBN 0 7506 0617 7

Library of Congress Cataloguing in Publication Data
A catalogue record for this book is available from the Library of
Congress.

Typeset by TecSet Ltd, Wallington, Surrey
Printed and bound in Great Britain by Biddles Ltd,
Guildford and Kings Lynn

Teaching and Learning:
A Guide for Therapists

Skills for Practice Series

Series editors: Sally French and Jo Laing

Titles published
  Practical Research: A Guide for Therapists
  Teaching and Learning: A Guide for Therapists
  Writing: A Guide for Therapists

In preparation
  Communication: A Guide for Therapists
  Human Relations in Helping: A Guide for Therapists

Contents

Preface

Over the past few years therapists have become more involved in teaching; the learners include undergraduate students, colleagues, carers and members of the general public. Despite this expansion of their role there is, at present, very little formal education available to practising therapists who wish to improve their teaching skills. Time to do so is also very limited.

The aim of this book is to provide a broad and practical guide to the many teaching methods available to therapists. These range from traditional methods, like the lecture, to those which involve considerable learner participation, such as role play, project work, seminars and discussion groups. Clinical teaching and teaching of practical skills are discussed, and the essential activities of preparation, assessment and evaluation are all examined. Although some attention is given to the processes of learning, the book is essentially a practical guide for the busy clinical therapist, rather than an in-depth treatise for a therapist undertaking a lengthy educational course. It is recognized throughout that for the adult learner, teaching and learning is a collaborative process, and that a successful and satisfying outcome is dependent on the interaction of what each has to offer.

Every effort has been made to ensure that the book is accessible to practitioners with no previous knowledge or experience of teaching. It may also be useful to experienced tutors who are keen to extend their expertise. The book is extensively referenced to assist those readers who require further information.

Thanks are extended to Caroline Makepeace for her help and encouragement, and to Jill Whitehouse for allowing us to use the following articles as the basis for some of the chapters:

French S. (1989) Teaching methods: 1. the lecture. *Physiotherapy* 75, 9, 509–10
French S. (1989) Teaching methods: 2. the discussion group. *Physiotherapy* 75, 10, 613–15
French S. (1989) Teaching methods: 3. student centred learning. *Physiotherapy* 75, 11, 678–80
French S. (1989) Teaching methods: 4. adding interest to your teaching. *Physiotherapy* 75, 12, 741–3

Most importantly of all, we would like to thank the many learners and teachers we have encountered over the years, without whose challenges, insights and encouragement we would never have developed the expertise or the confidence to write this book.

Sally French
Susan Neville
Jo Laing

Part One

Creating a Learning Environment

1

Helping People to Learn: Psychosocial Factors

Contemporary teaching practice is eclectic and based upon ideas and learning theories drawn from various schools of thought. Below is an outline of some of the major theories of learning.

Learning theories

Behaviourist theories of learning

The behaviourists view learning as resulting from stimulus–response connections. Beneficial responses to stimuli tend to be repeated and to become established, whereas harmful or unsuccessful responses tend to diminish or disappear. Thus learning can occur through trial and error and can be established through practice. It is also possible to influence the learning process by providing people with rewards and deterrents which shape their behaviour in given directions. Human beings are very sensitive to subtle signals of approval or disapproval and in this way can affect each other's behaviour and learning patterns. The behaviourists do not view the mental processes of the individual as important in the understanding of the learning process, but rather concentrate on observed behaviour.

Cognitive theories of learning

Cognitive learning theorists view the learner as an active processor of information. They are interested in learners' mental processes rather than their behaviour, and place great emphasis on prior knowledge, experience and assumptions. Over time existing knowledge and experience of a given subject area become organized into a mental framework, often referred to as a 'schema' or 'set'. People tend to interpret new events, assimilate new information, and approach new learning tasks in accordance with these schemata; for example, it will be less effort for therapy students to understand the pathological changes of multiple sclerosis if they have knowledge of the normal nervous system. The more complex the schema, the easier it is to understand, assimilate, interpret and remember new information of a similar kind.

Therapists need to be aware of the extent and complexity of the learner's existing schemata. This will vary from individual to individual even at the same stage of their education. It is easy to overestimate or underestimate people's knowledge; some people may feel inhibited about asking questions, whereas others may be reluctant to reveal considerable knowledge and expertise for fear of appearing boastful, or of causing embarrassment to the therapist. The therapist should aim to help learners enrich their knowledge by linking new with existing material, challenging prevailing ideas, and forming bridges between theoretical and practical information. The more links which are made the easier it is for the learner to remember the material. Thomas-Edding (1987) believes that teachers sometimes expect learners to organize and assimilate information as efficiently as they themselves do; once knowledgeable on a subject it is very difficult to remember or imagine ignorance or confusion.

Prior knowledge or an existing attitudinal 'set' may inhibit rather than enhance learning. People are motivated to maintain psychological balance and tend to resist knowledge if its incorporation gives rise to imbalance and the need to reorganize information and attitudes. If a piece of information or a treatment philosophy conflicts with an existing system of beliefs, the new knowledge may be rejected or distorted. Thus people do not merely assimilate material which is presented to them, but actively manipulate it. A dogmatic approach on the part of the therapist probably makes rejection of the ideas presented more likely.

The Gestalt theory of learning

Gestalt theorists believe that 'the whole is greater than the sum of the parts'. Just as a whole symphony is greater than the sum of the notes, so Gestalt theorists believe that mental processes, including learning, can only be comprehended in terms of their entirety. The concept of 'insight' is used by Gestalt theorists to describe the phenomenon whereby people experience a sudden flash of inspiration or understanding. They believe this occurs as a result of a rapid reorganization of the learner's experiences. Controversy exists regarding whether tasks should be learned by breaking them up into parts or leaving them whole. Gestalt theorists favour the latter approach, though Pask (1976) believes that the success of either strategy varies according to the individual's learning style.

Learning by observation and participation

It is possible to learn a task by watching others perform it, and this may be very helpful to the learner initially, but it is rarely sufficient in the learning of a new skill. People tend to learn best if they are actively involved, so it is important that learners are given sufficient opportunity to carry out tasks themselves, with help if necessary. Repetition to the point of over-learning is needed to become really proficient. Ford and Jones (1987) point out that skilled workers often have a tremendous urge to intervene when learners are attempting a new task and that this should be avoided as it increases the learner's dependency.

Transfer of training

Positive transfer of training from one task to another is said to occur when the earlier learning task facilitates the later learning task. Negative transfer is said to occur when the earlier learning task hinders the later learning task (Child, 1986). Rogers (1989) believes that training exercises can adversely affect performance of the real task unless the two are very similar. In general when two tasks are superficially similar though requiring different responses transfer of training is likely to be negative (Walkin, 1982; Child, 1986). Walkin (1982) points out that in educational tasks there are often elements of both negative and positive transfer.

If people learn to perform tasks inaccurately it can be more difficult for them to correct their responses than it would be for novices to learn the new skills. A person who has learned to type with two fingers, for example, will probably find it more difficult to learn the correct method than someone with no experience of typing. It is obviously important that therapists ensure that tasks are learned correctly the first time. (For further information on transfer of training, the learner is referred to chapter 12.)

Cognitive styles

Messick states that, 'Each individual has preferred ways of organizing all that he sees and remembers and thinks about' (1978: 4). These preferences are termed cognitive styles or learning styles.

Honey and Mumford (1982) devised a questionnaire which identified four cognitive styles, those of activist, reflector, theorist and pragmatist. The activist likes activity and new experiences, thrives on challenge and enjoys crises. The reflector, on the other hand, likes to ponder, is thorough and cautious and prefers to take a back seat. The theorist is rational, has a logical step-by-step approach to learning and is concerned with basic concepts. The pragmatist is eager to initiate action and likes to try out new ideas.

Most people have one or two preferred cognitive styles. No style can be said to be superior to any other but rather each is suited to different learning tasks or aspects of a task. Thus individuals may seek or avoid certain areas of learning or activity according to their preferred cognitive styles. Theorists, for example, may be loathe to apply their knowledge whereas pragmatists may not fully understand the basis of their actions. Although at first glance pragmatists may appear to suit the active role of the therapist best, all four styles are relevant to clinical or fieldwork practice.

Therapists will have their own preferred styles of learning and may find it difficult to help or respond positively or adequately to learners with different styles from their own. Honey (1988) concludes that people with all four styles within their repertoire are best equipped to teach but, unfortunately, only a minority of people are so versatile. Jobling (1987) believes that the more flexible teachers are with regard to their learning style, the more effective their teaching; however Reid (1984) contends that the teaching methods used have to be compatible with the personality of the teacher.

Therapists should to some extent adapt to the differing cognitive styles of learners; this can be achieved by varying the teaching methods used. It is also important for therapists to encourage learners to adopt a variety of cognitive styles as this will increase their overall effectiveness and versatility. The individual's preferred cognitive styles, though deeply rooted in personality structure, are not fixed and can be modified and extended.

Many other learning styles have been described. Hudson (1966) made the distinction between the 'converger' and the 'diverger'. Convergers enjoy thinking about technical impersonal matters and like arguments to be clearly defined and logical. They are not interested in probing into topics of a personal, emotional nature, nor in controversy. Divergers are the reverse, they enjoy controversy and uncertainty but are not interested in technical matters. Hudson found that convergers tend to specialize in physical sciences, whereas divergers favour the arts, law and business where decisions are made on the basis of probability. Beard and Hartley (1984) contend that divergers are difficult for teachers to cope with as they tend to think outside the learning structures provided for them.

Pask (1976) describes the 'holist' and the 'serialist'. Serialists like to take a step-by-step approach when solving a problem, whereas holists like to look at problems in their entirety. Another learning style is that of 'field dependence' versus 'field independence'. According to Messick (1978) the field independent person is able to isolate specific factors from their context, is analytical, and has an impersonal orientation. The field dependent individual, on the other hand, tends to view situations globally, lacks competence in analytic functioning, has a social orientation, and is socially skilled.

Only the minority of people tend to extremes, most showing a slight tendency to adopt some learning styles rather than others. All learning styles are beneficial in their different ways, their effectiveness varying according to the task.

The learner's state of mind

The state of mind of learners will have a large effect on their ability to learn, and the therapist will often be in a position to influence this. An important consideration is the learner's level of anxiety. Brown and Atkins (1988) believe that a non-threatening environment is essential if significant learning is to take place.

Trait anxiety, the individual's general tendency to be anxious, and state anxiety, the individual's level of anxiety in particular situations, though positively correlated, are distinct. Thus the environment can be modified to alter the anxiety level of the learner. The Yerkes–Dodson Law (1908) states that if arousal is either very high or very low, performance and the learning of complex tasks are adversely affected. This is illustrated in Figure 1.1:

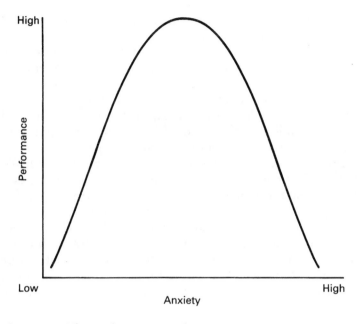

Figure 1.1 *The Yerkes–Dawson law*

If anxiety is too great learners are unable to concentrate and apply themselves to the task, and if it is too low they will tend to be apathetic and under-stimulated. The level of a person's anxiety is not always very easy to assess as various measurements – physiological, behavioural and self-report – tend to correlate poorly.

The task of the therapist is not to eliminate the learner's anxiety but to prevent it from becoming debilitating. The information given should be paced so that the learner is able to assimilate it and retain it. Probably the most important factor is for the therapist to create an atmosphere where learners feel able to ask questions even if they think they ought to know the answers or have been told before. This type of relationship is very helpful to therapists too as they will receive feedback which will enable them to understand learners' difficulties and limitations, as well as improve their own practice. On rare occasions learners may lack sufficient anxiety to stimulate action in which case it may be necessary to increase their level of anxiety a little.

Mason (1984) believes that the two major dimensions of successful teaching are understanding the subject matter to be taught, and the ability to create a learning environment and form relationships with learners. In a study by Neville and French (1991), student physiotherapists were most concerned that their clinical teachers should be friendly and approachable, a finding which tallies with other similar studies.

Any emotional problems learners may have are also likely to affect their performance adversely. Maslow (1943) believes that the desire to achieve intellectually and to reach one's full potential can only be realized when more basic needs are satisfied. He expressed this idea in terms of a hierarchy of needs where those needs at the bottom of the hierarchy, i.e. physiological, safety and social needs, must be satisfied before high-level needs, such as the need for intellectual achievement and self-fulfilment can be addressed. This is illustrated in Figure 1.2:

Figure 1.2 *Maslow's hierarchy of needs*

Although this model can be criticized (some people achieve a great deal despite tremendous odds) it is nevertheless useful.

Beard and Hartley (1984) point out that underachievement is caused by many factors unrelated to intellect, such as debilitating anxiety, emotional difficulties and a lack of security. The therapist should be aware that events in the lives of learners may bring about fluctuations in their ability to learn and should be prepared to counsel them if the need arises.

Motivation

The will to learn depends on internal motivators, for example interest, enjoyment or wanting to achieve, and external motivators, for example praise, money or passing examinations. External motivation has little effect if internal motivation is seriously lacking. Internal and external motivators do, of course, interact, for example being praised may increase the desire to succeed, and being paid for a task may increase its enjoyment. Thus although internal motivators tend to be more powerful, they may be enhanced or diminished by external factors. Although adult learners should, to a large extend, take responsibility for their own motivation and learning, the therapist is well placed to enhance their ability to do so.

If learners appear to be uninterested, unmotivated, or achieving poorly, there is a tendency to spend less time with them and to be more critical, with the possibility of worsening their state of mind and creating a vicious circle. It helps to remember that behaviour, including learning, is at least as much determined by the interaction between the individual's characteristics and the situation, as by the individual's characteristics alone (Argyle et al., 1982). Many psychologists and sociologists believe that the emphasis on the individual is an unfortunate misdirection of focus. Thus rather than counselling or criticizing the 'unmotivated' or 'uninterested' learner, it might be more constructive on occasions to examine the environment in which the learner is placed. The therapist is clearly a very important influence in determining the learners' environment, and is therefore in a key position to influence their motivation and learning.

Positive reinforcement

Motivation is increased by giving praise and encouragement when learners perform well; it is probably true to say that in British society we have a tendency to congratulate others, and ourselves, rather too infrequently. Positive reinforcement can enhance the individual's self-esteem which can have a large effect on achievement (Thomas, 1980). If praise is given it must be genuine or the learner will receive false feedback and may lose confidence and respect for the therapist.

Negative reinforcement

Negative reinforcement in this context refers to disapproval or failure to reward a response in order to eliminate it. Criticizing specific acts, or aspects of a task, can be effective in enhancing learning, but a general attitude of criticism and punitiveness is likely to affect the learner's motivational state adversely. Criticism should be related to specific problems which can be changed, rather than being directed at the learner's personality as a whole. It is unusual for a learner's performance to be wholly bad and criticism can be tempered with praise and suggestions for improvement.

Feedback

By giving reinforcement, either positive or negative, therapists provide valuable feedback to learners enabling them to improve their performance. Although improvement can occur without knowledge of results, it is greatly enhanced if feedback is provided. Feedback is most useful if given immediately and regularly, it can then be related to the behaviour it concerns and gives the learner the time and opportunity to improve before being assessed. Learners should always be given the chance to discuss or disagree with what is said about them, though they may need considerable encouragement before they are prepared to do so.

Success

Success is highly motivating and will facilitate learning, thus the therapist should attempt to ensure high levels of success in learners. The pace of learning should ideally be adjusted to suit each individual so that success is assured. As well as succeeding most people like to feel they are being stretched intellectually or there is a danger of boredom, thus a delicate balance must be struck.

Interest and enjoyment

Interest and enjoyment were cited above as internal motivators. High levels of interest and enjoyment can be achieved in many ways. The course material must be relevant to the learners and they may, at least in part, decide what the course or series of teaching sessions should contain. Active participation and a wide variety of teaching methods will help to ensure that interest and enjoyment remain high. If a number of therapists are involved in running a course, it is important that they communicate with each other and plan the course together or the learners may be subjected to the same teaching method, usually the lecture, time and again. A variety of therapists will also help to hold the interest of learners.

Competition and co-operation

Competing and co-operating with others can be highly motivating and can enhance learning. Co-operation is more relevant than competition in clinical and fieldwork teaching or when learners are working on a group project, but competition does have a place in education, for example when undertaking quizzes and educational games. Learners may sometimes set themselves the personal task of 'coming top', which may well motivate them, but it is usually inappropriate to advocate competition of this type. Therapists should instead encourage learners to improve their own skills and competences regardless of how others are performing.

Conclusion

Griffiths views teaching 'as a process of drawing out from within' and a teacher as a facilitator who is responsible for promoting or hastening the process of learning (1987: 335). Therapists may be asked to teach students or colleagues even though they have received little, if any, formal training. This may seem daunting, but it helps to remember that therapists, in their clinical role, are constantly engaged in teaching patients and clients and often do so in more difficult physical and psychological circumstances than college teachers encounter. Therapists who are asked to teach can therefore be assured that they have very many relevant skills at their disposal.

2

Helping People to Learn: Practical Factors

Before engaging successfully upon a teaching task, it is necessary for a therapist to have various areas of knowledge. For example, it is essential to know something of the background of those who are to be taught. A therapist will not teach a group of children in the same way as a group of colleagues and a third approach would be appropriate for a group of student therapists visiting the department.

An understanding of the intellectual processes of learners and of the subject in hand is, of course, invaluable to a therapist but a large part of the teaching and learning process pivots upon practical tasks to be undertaken by both therapist and learner. The learning process will be enhanced if steps are taken to ensure that these practical tasks are undertaken efficiently and in a way and to a timescale that suits all parties. As Curzon reminds us 'Teaching involves the provision of those conditions that directly promote effective learning' (Curzon, 1990: 3).

Such practical tasks might include, for instance, formal written tasks, practical tasks like learning to operate a piece of electronic equipment, background reading, or the retrieval of information. While each will be approached in the light of the learners' previous experience and the knowledge the therapist has of the way the learning is most likely to take place intellectually, each of these tasks has a practical aspect.

Environment

'Often, the very environment in which the class works acts as a "noise source" which interferes with and distorts reception of the teacher's message' (Curzon, 1990: 119). Even a traditional 'classroom' situation, where a therapist is imparting information by the spoken word perhaps, must be organized. Anything that interferes with the smooth flow of ideas back and forth or makes any of the participants uncomfortable will be stressful. As Marshall and Rowland (1989: 6) put it 'if you are relaxed you can learn more effectively.' The therapist will not enjoy working with a class who cannot concentrate. If the learners are not 'sitting comfortably' then they will not learn effectively. If the room is unpleasantly chilly, uncomfortably hot or plagued with a distracting background noise, then all will not be well. The room might be too big for the therapist to be heard properly or so small that it might prove impossible for all the learners to take notes. It is worth remembering that, if notes are to be taken, a flat surface is needed.

If the therapist wishes the learners to have brought equipment with them, then the learners should be aware of this expectation. It might be, of course, that the therapist wishes to provide the necessary equipment. In this case it should be to hand and in sufficient quantity to suit the needs of the activity proposed.

It might be that it is desirable to play the group a video or audio tape. In this case, the therapist should be familiar with the available equipment so that there are no distracting pauses. The therapist should also be quite certain that an audio tape, particularly, can be heard. Domestic cassette players are notoriously inaudible in large rooms where a group of well-clad persons are reducing the sound.

Even the most experienced of therapists should keep up routines of checking that the area to be used for teaching is available and suitably equipped even to small details. If, for example, the whole of the exercise hinges around a flip chart and marker pens, then the lack of them will render it disorganized and less than effective.

The fact that the therapist should be personally well prepared will be dealt with in detail in the next section of this book but it goes almost without saying that any degree of personal unpreparedness is immediately recognized by learners of all ages. If it is present, this deficit will not assist in cementing the good relationship between therapist and learners which is desirable for learning to take place.

The therapist should also be aware of the students' knowledge of the whole geography of the building in which they meet. A new learner attached to a therapy department, for instance, will need careful orientating, even in a relatively compact space.

The learners may be expected to use various facilities, for example reprographic, video or audio equipment. If this is the case then they will get more valuable use from these if they are clearly shown how they are to be used, not simply told that such facilities exist. A simple hand-out or instruction sheet can be very helpful, but few things are as useful as a little time spent showing how something is done. If the department is host to a group of learners who all need access to such facilities then it is often only necessary to show one or two of these how the equipment is used and this learning can be passed on.

The library

If learners are to engage in writing tasks or in retrieving information then they may wish to use a library. The term library may refer to an extensive, technologically catalogued collection or a few shelves holding books within a therapy department. The latter, though a humble offering, may be well worth mentioning to learners as what is contained there is likely to be very readily available and very salient to the task in hand.

Marshall and Rowland remind us that 'to use libraries fully, you need to know what materials they offer, learn how to gain practical access to the materials they contain, and learn how to find items in them' (1989: 74). Many libraries and large information centres in these modern times require users to be, to some degree at least, computer literate and not everybody is. Some people are very wary of the use of such equipment and may need encouragement and assistance to get the best use of these facilities.

Learners who are student therapists may have been given a thorough introduction to a large library and will, therefore, take the using of them in their stride. Queries may come to the therapist, however, from learners who are perhaps colleagues who have not had access to such new library technology. If this is the case it will be very useful to them if the therapist as teacher is acquainted with the various indices that a library catalogue might contain and the access points to them. They may be contained, for example, on cards, within a database or on a microfiche system.

It will be even more useful if the therapist has ideas about the best way of conducting library searches using a computer system, particularly if the learner can gain advice on the selection of key words for this purpose. Really valuable advice can also be given if the therapist is aware of other services that the library may provide, that of inter-library loan, for instance.

It is, of course, an old student adage, that the teacher will send fifteen students to a library to find indispensable reading which will invariably be contained in the library's only copy of a book which is out of print. It is necessary that the therapist, when expecting learners to be using a particular library, is familiar with those sections of it that are going to be of most use to them.

Most potential library problems can, in fact, be overcome before they arise if the learner is encouraged to use the services of the librarian who will know the library better than anyone. Most librarians are delighted to introduce their libraries to groups of users, if they are forewarned, and will explain layout, catalogue and computer systems. (For further and more detailed information on library use the reader is directed to Partridge and Barnitt, 1986 and French 1993.)

Tasks and their timing

It is very often the therapist who suggests useful tasks for learners and here practical considerations are important. It is firstly very necessary that instructions and suggestions are clear. It is better to say 'it would be helpful to read chapters 3 and 7 of that book, and chapter 16 if you have time' than 'this is a good book, you might have a look at it by next week'. It is also a demoralizing experience for learners if, after reading a recommended passage or book before a seminar or course day, there is then no perceivable link between their reading and the content of the learning experience. They will feel much more satisfied if what they have read is really used.

The importance of pace in teaching cannot be overstressed and the use of time and the organization of tasks within it is something that improves with experience. As a general rule, it is good practice to give learners as much warning as possible of timed tasks and the time at which they must be concluded. This goes for the ten-minute exchange of information where the instruction might be 'I'd like you to share your findings with a partner for ten minutes and then be prepared to tell the whole group what two things you both felt were most important' as well as the set essay where the title might be given six weeks before it is taken in for marking.

'Imposing one pace on a group is not an effective way for the group to learn' (Rogers, 1989: 45). A sensitive therapist will remember that learners will work at different rates and should seek to be sure to allow enough time, where possible, for tasks to be done. It is a great help to a learner to know how much time is available and so the way that the work is timetabled, overall, should be published. It helps to see in advance the pattern of an hour-long session or the practical work that will accompany a whole placement period.

Sometimes teachers, who themselves rarely engage in the tasks they set, insist on tasks being completed in a period of time that is totally unrealistic. If a large section of a group has not completed a task then the therapist should resist the temptation to think that they are all lazy but to consider if, for the majority of them, the task was impossible in the time allowed. Reading tasks, in particular, are very often set in an airy fashion that seems to suggest that it takes no time at all, perhaps because it is by and large a less onerous activity than many. However, reading and understanding several closely-worded chapters can take considerable time.

It is important to remember that realistic time should be allowed for preparatory reading. If a therapist is running a course which takes up a day for each of six consecutive weeks, then a whole reading list should be sent well in advance of the course; it would be helpful to learners also if, on such a list, the most important references were identified in some way. It will not, generally, be enough to give out a reading list one week for the next week's session to learners who, however keen they are, may be working full time as well as having home commitments.

Assessment and evaluation

Anyone who takes teaching seriously knows how important it is for learners to receive useful feedback on the tasks they complete. Such feedback is not only useful for learners who are in error or who have an incomplete grasp of ideas but also for a learner who has submitted an excellent piece of work, for there will still be points to be made which might make that piece of work even better. This could take the form of written comments or a 'talking through' of a task either in preparation or when completed. Such feedback should be non threatening, constructive, clear and, perhaps most importantly, prompt. If learners are left in ignorance of what they are doing wrongly then mistakes can be 'learned' and are therefore more difficult to erradicate. If feedback from, say, an essay is prompt, then the task itself is more likely to be clearly in the mind of both learner and therapist and the response will be more helpful.

But feedback should work both ways. It would be a very insensitive therapist who did not want to know what the learners thought of the learning experience provided. Much might be gleaned from informal discussion. However, it is a good thing to formalize some feedback. Learners can be asked to evaluate the teaching they have received in various ways with a written response, although usually they would not be asked to write at length. If the learning experience is very good or very unhelpful, then the feedback will probably come unbidden, but it is useful for a therapist who feels that a very 'ordinary' learning experience has been delivered, to elicit some feedback from the learners.

The therapist should also build in a personal system of evaluating the experience provided. The key question for the therapist is whether the learners are learning. Sometimes the therapist's evaluation, using that criterion, will not match at all that given by the learners. A therapist may feel, for example, that a videotape used in a session was very unclear in terms of getting important points across even though the group members might have had a most entertaining time at the session and may evaluate it highly on that basis. The evaluation could separate these factors by asking both how useful and how enjoyable it was.

The evaluation process, for both therapist and learner, is a practical way of summing up the effectiveness of what has happened and, perhaps more usefully, formalizing policy for the future. It is not, simply, a PR exercise in itself. Rogers writes that we use it 'to plan new strategies, make choices, establish priorities; to determine where we are in the teaching–learning process at present and what to do next; to identify helps and hindrances and decide what to do about them' (1986: 173). For further, more detailed, information on assessment and evaluation, the reader is referred to chapters 14 and 15.

Conclusion

Teaching involves the passing on of ideas or practical skills. We all think we can remember those teachers who, with no reference to notes, presented ideas or demonstrated skills in such a meaningful, fluid way that it was 'made easy'. We like to think that these 'born teachers' are the absolute epitome of their profession. This is, however, rarely the reality. Every effective teacher thinks about the tasks that learners need to undertake and, in effect, makes sure that they are able to do so.

Part Two

Preparation

Chapter

3

Knowing the Learners

One of the keys to successful teaching is, of course, meticulous planning. However, before a teacher's planning arrives at the stage of breaking down a body of knowledge into session-sized chunks, each with its individual aims, there are several very important general considerations regarding any particular teaching situation which need to be analysed so that various overall strategies can be considered before the bread and butter planning is undertaken.

Who are the learners?

Teaching is not, of course, something that is simply done to others. Education takes place only if someone is learning and any teacher needs to understand who those learners are. The answer for a therapist may be 'they are my colleagues within the hospital department or the students who are currently working with me.' While this is true it is only the beginning; it will be useful for the therapist, when working in the teaching role, to know rather more about the learners than this.

The stereotype that still exists of a student, for example, is of someone essentially young and inexperienced in the ways of the adult world. Many young students, though, may be able to bring considerable experience to their studies if permitted to do so. Age, gender and cultural backgrounds of students vary more widely than was the case even twenty years ago. With these differing backgrounds comes a range of experience. This variety has not always been recognized as a useful element. A rather unfortunate stereotype of mature students, for example, might present them as slower and less open to ideas than their younger counterparts. 'The older student' writes Curzon, 'will probably have experienced some deterioration in physical agility, in the activity of his senses, in certain abilities and in his short term memory' (1985: 168).

There is also a notion that older students feel more threatened than younger ones when asked to take on board concepts that might change long-established patterns of behaviour and thought. Curzon suggests that 'feelings of safety and security should not be attacked and destroyed; a mere perception of external threat to wellbeing will put older students on the defensive' (Curzon, 1985: 158).

Suppose the teaching is aimed at a therapist's colleagues in a hospital department. Here, also, the learners will bring a breadth of age and experience to that teaching session. Working lives may have taken those who currently work in a department through many different specialities, through departments at many hospitals with a variety of size, expectation and ethos.

Learners also bring to the learning situation their cultural backgrounds. Thus, a thirty-year-old working-class, white woman, with two schoolchildren, living on a suburban council estate, will bring to a course quite different expectations, knowledge and mores than the learner standing next to her who may be single, black, male, aged twenty-two, living in hostel accommodation, having recently arrived from West Africa and, in addition, may be working in his second language.

Other experiences which are brought to their studies by learners may also affect their perception of what they are taught. Learners may be disabled, may be carers or may recently have been therapy patients themselves. They may have just attained excellent 'A' level results or feel underconfident of what they perceive to be their low level of education. They may have easily made the transition from one educational institution to another or be quaking with remembered fear after twenty years out of a classroom. Any student may be bilingual, computer literate, possessed of a Heavy Goods Vehicle licence or all three.

The important thing, from the therapist's point of view, is that this panorama of experience within the group of learners should not be seen only as a problem but also as something that can be used to positive advantage. While there is, for example, some evidence to support the suggestion that older learners are less agile physically and may take a little longer to learn, there is also much to recommend them. They are, generally, very motivated and bring a more experienced view of the world to bear upon their learning. 'Older people see greater ambiguity and complexity in intellectual or social problems than they did when younger. Experience has taught them that easy answers are to be mistrusted . . . it can often be a great advantage to the adult learner when the teacher knows how to solicit and use the range of an adult's experience' (Rogers, 1984: 68). Similarly, it is highly likely that a learner who has brought up a family might bring very meaningful insight to the treatment of children, and someone who has lived in another part of the world might have useful information to impart regarding relative methods of treatment.

We learn by our experiences and so strategies for teaching a very mixed group ought to include activities to find out not only what the learners already know but also what they want to know. At the very least this can include the process commonly known as 'brainstorming' as an introduction to a particular topic. This is where known ideas about a topic are pooled orally and noted centrally, or where questions about a topic that members of a group require to be answered are similarly gathered together. This kind of session should also include encouragement to learners to talk about their views in an atmosphere that does not suggest to them that such views are unorthodox or ill informed.

It is the frequent experience of teachers that those who learn from them know much of what will be taught beforehand. This does not mean that teachers regularly find themselves redundant but rather that their role is to enable learners to set what they know into a context. All of us know a great deal that we have never been asked to verbalize. All of us know much about situations from our own points of view but often have not investigated them from the points of view of others. Teaching very often involves finding a means of pooling that knowledge so that a more complex structure for conceptualizing can be achieved by all. Rogers (1986: 11) refers to this process of education as 'a planned learning opportunity which one party provides for another in relation to an agreed objective.' This pooling of ideas can be a very liberating experience; it can be psychologically very satisfying for everyone in a teaching and learning group to realize that views and experiences are shared.

The overriding implication of the above is one which a therapist in the teaching role may find daunting. Strategies for teaching must be flexible. The best therapists will vary their approaches to what they are teaching as their knowledge of what the learners bring to the situation increases.

What do the learners need?

In addition to devising strategies to cope with who the learners are, the therapist should be very clear as to what the learners want and need to know. The learners may need to cover various aspects of a wider curriculum, they may need to be able to learn and perfect a particular technique, they may need just to orientate themselves within a particular area of the hospital or to become familiar with a particular piece of equipment. In all these cases, it is helpful if the therapist and learner are in agreement as to what should be the subject of learning. If learners are not clear as to how this learning fits in with the rest of their studies and practice then they may be confused, if for example they really have no idea why they are being bombarded with certain information, then they may become resentful. If there is a tacit agreement that what is being learned is useful, then things will proceed more smoothly than if not.

Most people engaged in teaching are, to an extent at least, agents. They are providing a conduit for knowledge and information from an academic institution, hospital, therapy department, examination board or equipment manufacturer to the learners. What these learners need to know will be, on the one hand, perceived by these institutions, indeed may be written down as a syllabus, a set of rules for practice, or, in the case of equipment manufacturers, operating instructions, in some detail. This kind of directive exists independently of both therapist and learner and both parties may have an acquaintance with those directives before they are acquainted with each other. The therapist is sure to have ideas about the way this information should be presented. The learners, on the other hand, will have ideas about what they need to learn and this is unlikely to be in exact accordance with what is suggested by the institution or the therapist. The effective therapist should be able to marry the body of knowledge concerned with the various sets of expectations.

Some needs may be perceived very similarly by all parties. 'I need to understand the function of the lungs or that exam will not be passed' or 'I need to know how to operate this piece of equipment so that I may treat Mr X'. In these instances the job of the therapist as agent is likely to be uncomplicated. Sometimes, however, ideas do not fuse so happily. 'Why do I need to learn this again when I feel I have already covered and assimilated this part of the curriculum?' or 'Why should I give up this lunch hour to learning when my prime need is to shop for my family's evening meal?' are far more difficult needs and perceptions to reconcile. It is sometimes the case, also, that conflict arises between subject areas or the thorny area of theory being translated into practice. For example, a sociology course may present a module for learning concerned with disability studies and this, in turn, may throw into doubt what has already been learned or what is practised in a particular department. It should be clear that timing in teaching is all important and that, as a general rule, it is more difficult to introduce controversial ideas during the later stages of a course.

It is necessary, to avoid problems of this kind, that at the outset of a course, in-service training session, or ten minute session with a piece of equipment, both therapist and learner discuss what they both hope will be learned by the end of it.

Clearly, if the educational endeavour is to cover some weeks then discussion in detail will be a useful activity. The teacher should be prepared to answer questions about content and approaches that can be negotiated and also to give details to the learner of expectations. This discussion and tacit agreement is sometimes referred to as a learning contract. It may, in some instances, be worth putting this in writing for future reference, alternatively it may just be stated in a couple of sentences. 'Before you go to lunch, we'll spend ten minutes looking at the ultrasound machine. We can make quite sure that you know how to use this particular model.' (For further information on learning contracts, the reader is referred to chapter 4).

In a longer course, this kind of exploration of need, expectation and progress should be a continuing feature of the teaching and learning process. As Rogers puts it, 'such a procedure enables us to test the assumptions we have made and to amend the proposed schedule of work in the light of this reassessment; and it enables the participants to alter the pattern of work proposed, to adjust their expectations if necessary' (Rogers, 1986: xxxiii).

All this being said, it should also be remembered that many learners come to an educational experience with a very clear, if individual, idea of what they need. The learning that they then do reflects and fulfils that need even if it is not what was perceived, either by an institution or the teacher, to be the need that the learner had. For example, a physiotherapy student may be required to complete a first degree course in order to be permitted to take postgraduate qualifications on the way to achieving an ambition to become a physiotherapy lecturer or a veterinary physiotherapist.

It is, however, often no less valid for all that. Most people engaging in a learning experience voluntarily are, to some degree at least, receptive to new ideas or will find a way of dealing with those which they find intolerable, but conflict can arise if, for example, a learner had perceived a course to be essentially concerned with learning practical skills and was then expected to learn a large number of skills concerned with communicating with patients or clients. This can, at its worst, result in a total impasse.

It should be mentioned here that some learners may have very particular needs that must be addressed. A wheelchair user will need access, a foreign or a deaf member of the learning group may need translation, a partially-sighted member may need overhead projector plates or handouts photocopied and enlarged. Needs such as these are often not difficult to fulfil but cannot be addressed at the last minute and a really effective teacher should be aware of them well before the teaching itself begins.

Constraints

All teaching occasions are constrained in some way or another from being ideal. The better these constraints are anticipated, then the better the fine planning and ultimately the teaching will be overall.

There are, of course, practical considerations. These may have to do with group size; a class of two is altogether different to plan for than one of fifteen. The therapist must also consider the time available for teaching. Is there, for instance, an allocation of several sessions with colleagues to pass on information regarding the course just attended, or merely half of one lunch hour? If there is to be more than one session, are these sessions close together so that skills can be built upon, or so far apart as to make the need for revision time to be accommodated within the planning?

The place where the learning takes place will vary and will affect planning. If a large group of people is expected to split into small discussion groups, or if the use of role play is planned, then the physical surroundings must accommodate these elements comfortably or it is better not to plan for them. The time of day that is allocated to the learning may be very important also. Colleagues will react very differently to being taught in the early morning than they might at the end of a long, hard working day. Certain kinds of learning programme might call for various items of equipment and this is another potential constraint as equipment often takes room, is shared, or has to be stored.

The venue for teaching often dictates the atmosphere in which the learning is to take place. If, for example, a therapist is teaching colleagues and using the space that the whole department regularly uses for eating and drinking and socializing then too much formality will seem strange. Learning situations can vary from the extremely formal to the highly informal. This will also depend upon the size of group, the social situation that exists within the group and perhaps the amount of information that is to be got through within a certain time. Clearly the larger a group, even if the group members are well known to each other, the more formal the presentation is likely to be. Conversely, if the group is very small, say just two students learning from a department member, then even if, up to the point of the beginning of the teaching session, they had no knowledge of each other at all, they might be on first name terms within three minutes. Bearing all this in mind, it will be wise for therapists to negotiate the best possible venue, even if this takes time.

Teaching method will also be matched to underlying aims. If the aim of a teaching session is simply to impart information as quickly as possible, then a session styled as a lecture might be appropriate. If, on the other hand, a discussion session is envisaged with a view to attitude change among the participants then something quite different will be necessary. (Individual teaching methods are discussed in subsequent chapters.)

Therapists should also consider their own personal approaches to teaching. All who teach have their individual strengths and weaknesses and while everyone hopes to improve with time, practice and experience it may be that some approaches are always more comfortable to use than others. There are various ways in which teachers can impede learning, some of them emanating from acquired habits barely noticed by those who have acquired them. In this regard Curzon warns 'an aggressive manner, a nervous disposition . . . the proto-linguistic signs which are swiftly interpreted by students as evidence of hostility or lack of interest in the subject matter, may block the pathway to learning' (Curzon, 1985: 76). For all these reasons, it is desirable that a system which allows learners to evaluate what they are being taught should be set up alongside the teaching, and that the results of such a system should be acted upon.

Conclusion

Therapists should always remember that the prime purpose of teaching is to communicate ideas and to allow and assist others to do so. Therapists' own knowledge, experience and attitudes and those of the learners, will shape this communication process as will constraints of time, place and availability of resources. While constraints are often regretted, their effects can be minimalized if strategies to accommodate them are adopted. It is essential for therapists in a teaching role to acquaint themselves with the learners both before they arrive and as the teaching progresses and that acquaintance should include a knowledge of what the learners will bring to the process as a whole.

4

Planning the Teaching Programme

Demands on a therapist's time to teach may be many and varied; the therapist may, for example, be asked to give a series of lectures to pre-qualified learners, or make a single presentation at a multidisciplinary meeting. Other requests could involve the teaching of practical skills to carers at a workshop, or clinically supervising qualified practitioners who are undertaking a refresher course prior to returning to work. Often such demands are additional to the usual work of the therapist.

Planning the proposed teaching is an essential requirement for success; it is all too easy for therapists to think that this can be done quickly since they are fully familiar with the subject matter. Planning is, however, a time-consuming process and the presentation of material in the most appropriate and efficient way dictates that time must be set aside. It may be helpful to consider the following four questions during the planning phase:

(1) What is the aim of the proposed teaching?
(2) How will the aim be achieved?
(3) How will the learning be assessed?
(4) How will the teaching and learning be evaluated?

Newble and Cannon (1983) suggest that the key to good planning is to develop educationally sound and logical links between aims, teaching and learning methods, and assessment procedures.

Identifying the aim

Considerable thought needs to be given to the purpose of the proposed teaching. This will necessitate consultation with those who have requested the teaching, perhaps colleagues, managers or academic tutors. It is important to understand how the proposed teaching will fit into the whole programme, to know what has gone before and what is likely to follow. Is the teaching part of a series, or a 'one-off' presentation? It is also important to know if and how the learning will be assessed and evaluated even if the therapist is not involved in these activities. With this knowledge to the fore, the next step is to formulate some aims which will encapsulate the purpose of the teaching programme. Examples might be:

(1) To understand a range of speech pathologies.
(2) To develop clinical competence.
(3) To understand the role of the occupational therapist in the intensive therapy unit.

Aims are general statements which serve to establish a direction for teaching (Jaques, 1991), but it is also necessary for the therapist to consider what the learners should accomplish. Clear statements of learning outcomes are called objectives and these should be identified in the light of the aims.

Writing learning objectives

Learning objectives are not easy to formulate clearly but time spent devising them will help to focus the teaching programme so that it is tailored to the learners' needs. It may be helpful to enlist some colleagues, or the learners themselves, to identify what is realistic. It is important to find out who the learners are and what abilities they already have (see chapter 3), as well as the specific outcomes that they desire. In addition, it is necessary to consider the available resources in terms of the therapist's time, technological support, space and equipment. Once these factors are known, it should be possible for the therapist to define more precisely what learning outcomes may be achieved (Curzon, 1990).

Let us imagine that the therapist has been asked to address a group of pre-qualified learners with the following aim: *To understand the role of the physiotherapist in the management of the elderly client in the community*. Learning objectives, in terms of what the learners need to be able to achieve, could include the following:

(1)   Describe the make-up of the primary health care team.
(2)   Outline the relevant legislation and social service provision.
(3)   Analyse and explain the needs of the client group.
(4)   Discuss the specific skills which the therapist may be called upon to provide.
(5)   Explain the interdisciplinary nature of the total management programme.

There is much debate about how objectives should be written. If they define a precise activity such as 'discuss' or 'analyse', as illustrated above, this facilitates the choice of a teaching and learning method, as well as the assessment procedure. However, an over-dependence on such behaviourist terms could limit the scope of the teaching programme and stifle the more imaginative and creative thinking that could emerge. (The reader is referred to Jaques, 1991 and Curzon, 1990 for fuller considerations of the arguments.)

On balance, where a body of knowledge needs to be acquired and a standard of competence achieved within the constraints of time and resources, it is important to devote some thought to defining learning objectives; indeed it is an essential aspect of the planning phase. The detail in which the learning objectives are expressed is the choice and responsibility of the individual therapist and, where appropriate, the learners themselves.

Selecting the teaching method

Once the learning objectives have been written, the next step is to consider which teaching method or methods to adopt. The number of learners in the group, the purpose of the teaching programme, the expertise and preference of the therapist, and the available resources, should all be known to enable the therapist to make an informed choice (Bligh et al., 1981). The needs of disabled learners in the group should also be considered; it may, for example, be necessary to ensure access for wheelchair users, or to organize an interpreter or note-taker for those with hearing impairments. If the therapist anticipates using patients or clients in the teaching programme, however, then planning should take into account a number of other factors.

Patients and clients are usually remarkably willing to participate in teaching sessions and it is important not to abuse their co-operation (Thompson et al., 1988). It is not only courteous but essential to get their consent first and not to over-use them or press them to participate, especially if they are particularly vulnerable. It is the responsibility of the therapist to be aware of the ethical requirements of using patients or clients as part of the teaching programme. If in-patients are being used it is necessary to check that they will not be wanted elsewhere, for example at a ward round, clinic or with their visitors. The ward manager should know exactly where the patients are, and how long they will be away from the ward. It is a useful strategy to have at least one other patient as a reserve in case the first should be unexpectedly unable to take part.

The use of equipment may also entail more planning than anticipated, particularly if it is to be borrowed. Permission may need to be sought in the first instance, and it is important to ensure that it will not be required elsewhere during the teaching session. The transportation of such equipment must also be considered, especially if it is not easily portable. If audio-visual aids are to be used these will either need to be prepared or acquired beforehand. (For a full discussion of audio-visual aids, the reader is referred to chapter 5.)

It can be helpful to use more than one teaching method within a teaching session in order to keep the interest of the learners alive. It is necessary to be flexible and sensitive to the learners' responses; the therapist's plans may fail to produce the desired results which may necessitate a change of method. In a series of teaching sessions the learners may progress more or less quickly than anticipated, so changes will need to be made to the original plan. These points highlight the need to evaluate the teaching and learning continuously. In relation to each specific teaching method it is useful to state clearly the aims at the beginning, and to summarize the major points covered at the end.

If the learning is going to be assessed, it is important that the assessment and teaching methods are compatible otherwise the learning will be compromised (Newble and Cannon, 1983). For example, theoretical knowledge may be taught at the expense of skills practice if a written examination is used as the assessment tool. In this situation the learners may, understandably, be less than willing to spend a great deal of time practising the skill. If, on the other hand, the learners are ignorant of the assessment requirement, they may fail the examination. This highlights the importance of knowing the assessment procedures when planning the teaching programme. (For a full discussion of assessment, the reader is referred to chapter 14).

Planning is not necessarily just the responsibility of the therapist; collaboration may take place between the therapist and the learner, depending on the purpose of the proposed teaching. An example of such collaboration is the use of the learning contract.

Negotiating a learning contract

Negotiating a learning contract demands an input from both the therapist and the learner where they discuss together the learner's needs. This is particularly useful if the therapist is supervising fieldwork or clinical practice. It requires the identification of learning objectives but goes further in that learning resources and assessment procedures are also specified (Gibbs, 1988). Such a contract might include the following headings:

Learning objectives (What do I want to learn?)
Learning resources (How will I learn?)
Assessment (Who will assess the learning? By what standards will the learning be judged?)

Time will need to be set aside for this activity which should ideally take place in the early days of the practice experience; it can then act as a guide for the remainder of the practice. It requires both the therapist and the learner to think carefully about what is required and what is available. An example of a learning contract is illustrated in Figure 4.1.

Learning objective: 'What do I want to learn?'

To perform an assessment of a client's home needs prior to discharge from hospital.

Learning resources: 'How will I learn?'

Accompany therapist on home visit, assist therapist, discuss findings with therapist, read college notes and relevant texts, carry out a minimum of two home visits under supervision, record findings.

Assessment: 'Who will assess the learning?'

Therapist will observe home visit assessment and read written report. I will review my own performance.

'By what criteria will the learning be judged?'

Comprehensive and logical sequence, adequate communication, accurate measurements, justification of client's needs, knowledge of what can be offered, feeling of confidence, clients/carers demonstrate trust in me. A full, legible and relevant written report.

Figure 4.1 *A learning contract*

In this example the objective is a concise statement of the desired learning and the criteria by which the learning will be judged: this will help to direct the learner and the therapist. The criteria should be written in sufficient detail to give absolute clarity to what is required, and the therapist and the learner should be in agreement. It is desirable, particularly with adult learners, to involve them in the learning process (Higgs, 1992). They should be encouraged to be critical about their own practice, thus introducing an element of self-assessment into the written contract.

An obvious worry could be the time involved in writing such a detailed contract. However, if the therapist and the learner put some thought into the matter beforehand this will accelerate negotiations when they come to produce the agreement. Windom (1982) suggests that the process of developing a contract is one of its strengths, thus time spent on it is not wasted.

Rehearsal

An aspect of the planning phase which is often neglected is that of rehearsal. If the therapist has done very little teaching then rehearsal is essential in order to achieve a good standard of presentation. Rehearsal may include such activities as running through the talk to check that the timing is right, tape-recording oneself and listening to the play-back, or getting a colleague to listen and check for any inappropriate or over-used phrases. If a colleague watches the rehearsal, then any annoying behaviours can be pointed out, for example pacing to and fro can be very off-putting, and talking done while writing on the blackboard or pointing to the screen becomes almost inaudible to the audience. Familiarizing oneself with the audio-visual equipment, and experimenting with the layout of the room may also be time well spent.

It may be helpful for the therapist to draw up a plan of the teaching session to be undertaken indicating the methods to be used, how long each part might last, and in what sequence the material will be delivered. This is illustrated in Figure 4.2.

Topic	Method	Time	Evaluation
Introduction	Talk	3 mins	
Possible client problems	Buzz groups & feedback	7 mins	
Example of a case study	Video	10 mins	
Summary of problems	Talk	3 mins	
Therapist's role	Small group discussion	10 mins	
"	Feedback	10 mins	
Conclusion	Talk	3 mins	

Figure 4.2 *Teaching method plan*

Presenting a plan such as this can act as a form of mental rehearsal. This can be very helpful especially if a practice session is not possible. An evaluation column encourages the therapist to evaluate the teaching session and to consider any changes which might need to be made on another occasion. (For a full discussion of evaluation, the reader is referred to chapter 15.)

How learners can plan

A number of references have already been made to how learners can and should be involved in the learning and planning process. The ways in which learners can help themselves can be made clear at the beginning of a teaching programme, particularly if it is to cover a number of teaching sessions.

A teaching programme is often part of a larger academic undertaking. It is necessary for the learners to make sure they are up to date with any prior learning on which the new programme will build. This is particularly important in the case of fieldwork experience, clinical practice and practical skills where previously-learned theory will be applied. The therapist needs to make sure that the learners know what is expected of them; this information can be given via the person who requested the therapist's input. The therapist may also have identified some pre-course reading which will need to be given to the learners in advance of the teaching.

Unexpected difficulties

Curzon speaks of a classroom with 'its unpredictable nature, its many instabilities and transient features' (1990:123). Even those therapists whose organization is painstaking will come across occasions when their preparation has not been enough. This will sometimes happen at the beginning of a session when the learners are an unknown quantity, or if a discussion point veers off on an interesting but unprepared for tangent. It is as well to remember that, generally, the less structured and more open-ended the method used for teaching, the more risks the therapist is taking. If, therefore, the therapist plans to use a very open-ended discussion, background knowledge of the area being taught will probably need to be greater than if, for example, the lecture is to be used.

If therapists find themselves in uncharted intellectual or organizational waters, it is always best to 'come clean'. A therapist when teaching should be prepared to say 'I don't know the answer but I'll find out' or 'You are right, I don't think this particular exercise is going to work even though I was sure it would.' Or even 'What a good idea, I had not thought of that.' It is, in fact, satisfying rather than threatening when learners begin to gain confidence in their own abilities and race ahead.

Expeditions

If therapists are involved in teaching the same learners over several weeks, they may decide to organize an expedition of some kind. As well as being beneficial educationally, expeditions can give a welcome lift to routine day-to-day teaching. The nature of these will vary: it may be that a therapist feels that learners would benefit from viewing an art exhibition produced by people with learning difficulties, or a theatre production that deals with the theme of terminal illness or old age. A local museum might house an exhibition exploring genetics, comparative anatomy, or medical history. The therapist might encourage learners to attend or, alternatively, a visit could be arranged more formally.

It is wise for therapists to gather as much information as possible about the event in advance to ensure it is really worthwhile. Theatres, cinemas and museums are usually more than ready to publicize their events and many operate regular mailing lists for a modest fee.

Team teaching

Rather than working alone, therapists may decide to plan and deliver their teaching sessions or programmes in partnership with their colleagues. This is known as team teaching which is said to operate, 'where two or more teachers co-operate deliberately and methodically in the planning, presentation and evaluation of the teaching process.' (Curzon, 1990: 302). Teams may be very small, consisting perhaps of just two people. If, for example, two members of a therapy department have attended a course and are responsible for imparting the knowledge to colleagues, they may opt to teach together. Success depends on co-operation and the acceptance of group responsibility; team members must have agreed objectives and be committed to the team approach. If several teachers are merely working together this does not, in itself, constitute team teaching.

Team teaching is valuable because expertise in both subject matter and teaching methods can be pooled. Many new ideas and perspectives can be gained from colleagues and immediate feedback received from them. As Curzon states:

> An important basic assumption made by some advocates of team teaching is that where teachers focus their collective attention on an instructional problem, the solution at which they arrive will probably be superior to those presented by the same teachers considering the same problem in isolation. Put quite simply 'two heads are often better than one.' (Curzon, 1990: 301)

The presence of supportive colleagues can also give therapists the confidence to attempt new techniques and teaching methods. It is likely too that the learners will benefit as the subject matter and views presented, as well as the teaching styles, will be more varied. Learners will see that there are many ways of viewing a topic and that the 'experts' do not always agree. Team teaching can be more democratic than conventional teaching and, if used well, can reduce both planning and preparation time as the labour is divided.

There are, however, some disadvantages. The main drawback is that team teaching is expensive in terms of time and money as more teachers are involved both in planning and delivery. A further problem is that the presence of several therapists may lead to a diffusion of responsibility, or certain team members may dominate while others conform (Brown, 1988). Therapists with greater knowledge, expertise or confidence must be careful not to stifle the ideas of other team members. Teams are really only as good as the relationships which exist between their members, but this having been said, therapists should not be frightened of some degree of conflict as this can lead to a more interesting and innovative teaching experience than that which may result from a very harmonious team.

Conclusion

Thorough planning of all aspects of the teaching programme will not only reduce anxiety but will enhance the therapist's confidence. The learners will also benefit if the therapist is organized and well informed. Teaching and learning are, however, unpredictable processes and, although a detailed plan is both necessary and useful, the therapist must be prepared to modify or even abandon it as the teaching session progresses. The willingness to do so may only come as experience and confidence are gained.

5

Preparing and Using Audio-Visual Aids and Handouts

The essence of teaching is to facilitate learning and the therapist, as well as considering a range of teaching methods, might usefully employ some form of visual or auditory aid in order to stimulate and maintain the learners' interest. Audio-visual aids have become more readily accessible in today's climate of advancing technology, and indeed learners not only expect their use but they anticipate a high standard of presentation. There is a wide range of aids from which to choose and the therapist will need to make an informed choice in the light of the purpose of the teaching session, the identity of the learners, their number and the availability and cost of the necessary resources.

Audio-visual aids should be seen as an integral part of the learning process if they are to be used to greatest effect (Cox and Ewan, 1988). It is important to realize that time and effort will be required particularly if the aids are to be made rather than bought. Cull (1986) suggests that first and foremost aids should be used when it is difficult or impossible to communicate the information by words alone, and secondly, they should be seen as enhancing the communication process. They can help learners to organize both their thinking and their note-taking but, like teaching methods, variety is necessary otherwise their use can become monotonous.

Therapists could decide to offer some form of handout or they might choose to show material using the overhead projector. Slides can be used to present text or the realities of practice, while audio tapes, tape slides and video recordings, which combine both commentary and visual images, may be an even greater adjunct to teaching. However, it is important not to neglect the use of the less sophisticated blackboard, whiteboard or flipchart, and examples of equipment, models and posters are also worthy of consideration.

When preparing audio-visual aids from whatever source, it is essential to abide by any copyright legislation. If patients are to be used, then it is also imperative to take account of ethical considerations. The use of patients as teaching material raises the dilemma regarding the respect of an individual's privacy on the one hand, and, on the other, the acknowledgement that using patients is for the common good and ultimately may benefit the patient through the increased knowledge gained (Thompson et al., 1988). However, each view needs to be tempered by the other and written informed consent should always be obtained.

Finally, if technical equipment is involved then it is also wise to test the equipment first to check not only that it is in good working order, but to make sure that material presented will be clear, legible and, if appropriate, audible as well. Lighting in the proposed teaching environment may need to be adjusted or the positioning of such things as the overhead projector, slide projector or screen may need to be tried out to make sure that the learners' vision will not be obscured. Sometimes it may be necessary to organize a technician to work the equipment, or the therapist may choose to operate it and will therefore need to be familiar with it.

Handouts

The term handout is a blanket term, referring to almost any printed matter handed individually to learners which does not usually stand on its own but is to be read in tandem with the therapist's presentation. Handouts will enable more material to be disseminated. Having a handout can relieve learners of notetaking and thus free them to become more receptive during the teaching session. Afterwards the handout is available for future reference and can thus aid revision of the topic.

The essence of a good handout is simplicity and there are several ways in which a handout should be simple. It should be easily read in a visual sense; a cramped, handwritten, poorly-photocopied sheet of A4 will not inspire confidence. Judicious use of headings, underlining, bold print, italics, all possible in today's atmosphere of familiarity with word processors and laser printers, will help in this respect. The contents should be easily understood and readily linked to the learning experience that they accompany. If the overhead projector is being used then photocopies of the transparencies can be given to the learners to enable them to concentrate on what is being said, making additional notes if necessary. The therapist should guard against putting too much information on the handout. There is not enough time to read full transcripts of lectures during the teaching session and such handouts are often filed away and forgotten. A much more appropriate kind of handout is one which identifies the salient points leaving space for the learners to write more as the session continues. A wide margin could be left at the right-hand side for this writing and space could also be left at the bottom to enable learners to make notes of questions asked, answers given and any additional points that may have been made during discussion. It might be appropriate to give handouts of diagrams which would take too long to copy, the learners might be asked to label them and make additional points of clarification.

Time which is saved by producing a handout can usefully be employed in discussion, seeking out the learners' opinions and making sure they have understood what has been said.

Finally, information can be included on the handout which directs the learners to further resources. No lecture or seminar can possibly contain all that the therapist wants to say, and indeed for some learners further information will be inappropriate. However, for others, a general lecture on a topic might lead to a more specific interest, and so a useful list of books, journal articles, pamphlets, videos etc. could be offered.

As photocopiers are so generally used these days, it is tempting to copy any articles or diagrams which may have relevance, but apart from the requirement not to abuse copyright, it is better to provide learners with material which is tailored exactly to the knowledge which the therapist wishes to impart. (For further information on copyright, the reader is referred to French and Sim, 1993.)

Overhead projectors

Overhead projectors are now in common use and it is unusual to find a teaching department without one. They may be used with or without a screen since it is possible to project successfully onto a plain, light-coloured wall. The acetates or transparencies are relatively cheap to buy and it is quite easy to make one's own 'overhead'. Pens come in a range of colours which may be washable or permanent. The use of washable colours has the advantage that corrections and adjustments can be readily made but there is the tendency for the transparency to become smudged if not handled carefully. The use of permanent colours, on the other hand, means that the transparency can withstand rougher handling but is less readily altered, although it is possible using a spirit-based solution.

   The main points of the teaching session may be presented, or diagrams which would otherwise take too long to draw on the blackboard, can be shown. Legibility and clarity are of prime importance. Newble and Cannon (1983) offer the following pointers:

(1)   Smallest printing should be no less than 5 mm letters.
(2)   Blue, black, brown and green show up particularly well, while red, orange and yellow are often difficult to see.
(3)   Reduce tabulated data to essential figures or use a graph.
(4)   Keep the transparencies simple, do not overcrowd with text or show too complex a diagram.

It is also worth remembering that lower-case lettering is easier to read than upper-case lettering, although the latter can be used for emphasis.

It is important to give the learners time to assimilate what is on the transparency and to copy it if appropriate. It can be useful to uncover the transparency step by step, using a sheet of paper which projects black. A pen or pencil laid across the transparency will act as a black marker, and can be used to draw the learners' attention to each point in turn. Another way of controlling the quantity of information on show is to build up the transparency using a series of 'overlays'. This process could be used to demonstrate, for example, an aspect of anatomy or the involvement of the multidisciplinary team in patient care. Each layer of transparency is attached to the top, bottom or sides of the original transparency, and the diagram can be assembled by superimposing these when needed.

Special transparencies are produced for use with the photocopier so that a printed sheet can be copied ready for the overhead projector, thus enhancing the standard of presentation. Similarly, diagrams from textbooks may be transferred in this way though the source of information must be acknowledged. X-rays and CT scans can also be projected successfully and are often more easily seen by a larger audience than when a viewing box is used.

The overhead projector can also be used as a substitute blackboard, so that ideas from a group of learners can be written down as they are received. The advantages over the blackboard or flipchart are that the therapist is always facing the learners and the transparencies, complete with ideas, may be taken away or copied.

Slides

Slides provide greater scope for the therapist to present aspects of practice which may complement any lecture or presentation. Provided resources are available for taking the photographs and producing the slides, then seeing slides of patients or equipment or surgical procedures often adds an element of realism which will enable the learner to understand more readily.

Slides may also be used to present text or tables of data resulting, for example, from a piece of research. Concern with clarity and legibility, mentioned in the previous section on overhead projectors, is equally important here. Cull (1986) suggests that the 7 × 7 × 7 rule is useful for text. This refers to the ideal maximum number of words in a title, lines of text on a slide and words in a line. In relation to tables, four columns is the ideal maximum while six columns are possible in a histogram or bar chart, but no more than three lines or curves should be presented on a graph.

Choice of colour is another aspect to be considered and the inclusion of coloured slides such as white text on a blue or green background can break up the monotony of black and white slides. However, slides, particularly coloured ones, are relatively expensive to produce. It is worth investigating what can be obtained from the on-site audio-visual department and to seek advice from the experts.

When presenting slides, if the same slide needs to be referred to more than once, then it is better to have a duplicate slide(s) in the carousel than to go back and find the original. This not only saves time but it will keep the continuity of the presentation. It is important to remember that room lighting has to be turned down for slides to be used effectively, thus making it difficult for learners to write. This will also inhibit questioning and it is useful to leave some time at the end of the presentation for this activity.

Audio tapes

Audio tapes are less often used than slides, but they do have a place, particularly when teaching the skill of interviewing or explaining disorders of speech. Tape and cassette recorders are so readily available that learners may be able to bring their own for the purpose of recording each other practising, for example, the type of questioning that may be adopted with specific client groups. It is so easy to slip into the use of jargon or to ask too many leading questions and the skill of being able to change one's language to suit the situation needs to be developed. Such activity also heightens the learners' perceptions of the extent to which the tape recorder (like the video camera) may inhibit the responses being sought. Being able to listen to a tape recording of the interaction between a skilled practitioner and client which could then be analysed provides an invaluable learning experience. Being able to listen to the speech of people with dysphasia or dysarthria will also be much more meaningful than if the therapist tries to imitate them.

Audio tapes can also be used by therapists as a means of evaluating their own teaching (Ashcroft et al., 1990). Recording a teaching session will provide a record from which the therapist may identify such aspects as variety of teaching methods used, timing of activities, depth and breadth of content and clarity of communication.

Tape slides

Tape slides, where a commentary accompanies a series of slides, are readily available commercially and it is possible to register with a company on a hire basis as well as being able to buy. Such a company is Graves Educational Resources which has an extensive collection suitable for health professionals. While a tape slide may be appropriate at the beginning of a teaching session, when questions could be asked of the therapist after watching the presentation, an additional use is for individual study when the learner can go through the sequence again at a suitable pace. In addition to tape slides, the above company also offers slide programmes and videotapes for hire or purchase. With all such teaching aids it is necessary for the therapist to be very familiar with their content before using them as a teaching medium as they often show only some of what is required.

Videotapes

Videotapes have become increasingly popular as a teaching medium. Not only can recordings be made of practical demonstrations but the video recording may be used to bring into the teaching environment many aspects of practice. This, of course, presupposes that the necessary equipment and expertise are available for making the video. Ashcroft et al. (1990) point out that unless a video recording is particularly well constructed, it is advisable to use only small sequences interspersed throughout the teaching session, otherwise watching uninterrupted video can lead to learners becoming passive and 'switching off'.

Another source of material is the television and many audio-visual departments will store on video suitable programmes as long as the staff are given sufficient advanced warning. The scope of video for enhancing the learning activity is wide and Newble and Cannon (1983) offer the following uses:

(1)   To introduce learners to a topic.
(2)   To provide a major source of information.
(3)   To stimulate discussion.
(4)   To give feedback on performance.

In introducing a topic, the therapist will want to stimulate interest and giving an overview is a way of doing this before looking at the material in greater depth. The physiotherapist, who wants to introduce gait analysis, may usefully show short extracts on video of different walking patterns while the speech and language therapist, who is concerned to explain how dysphasia may be alleviated, could show a series of short sequences of one or two patients speaking, at the beginning of their therapy, during their course of treatment, and prior to discharge.

As a major source of information, video recordings could be taken of therapy experts assessing or treating patients. Specialist areas of practice which are not readily accessible to learners could also be filmed, or learners could be introduced to the roles of other team members through the medium of video. Some recordings could be part of a teaching session but they would also be useful for learners to see on their own as revision material. Commercially-produced videos and copies of programmes from the television could also provide substantial amounts of learning material. However, it must be remembered that this requires the educational institution (or the audio-visual aids department) to have an educational recording agency licence.

The use of video in the form of 'trigger points' is especially conducive to stimulating discussion. The occupational therapist might want to cover such issues as ageism, sexism, racism, disabilism and death and bereavement. All these can be readily explored by exposing the learners to examples on video and then asking them to examine their own attitudes and emotional responses. If this is done in small groups, learners come to hear a range of opinions which may assist them in understanding not only themselves but the reactions and behaviour of their patients and clients.

A further use of video is to improve the performance of both the learners and the therapist. Colleagues could record each others' performances, whether practising a manual skill, using a piece of equipment, interviewing or presenting information. Immediate feedback helps the learner or the therapist to identify improvements which need to be made. Where possible, a video library could be compiled which would be accessible both to learners and therapists.

Blackboards, whiteboards and flipcharts

The use of blackboard and chalk is possibly the cheapest visual aid available to the therapist and it has the advantage that information can be presented in a gradual manner. It is also a useful medium for recording ideas from learners. A disadvantage is the fact that the therapist will need to turn away from the learners while writing but this is usually not a problem if only the main points of the teaching session are recorded. For therapists who find it difficult to write legibly or quickly with chalk, the marker pen used on a whiteboard may be easier to handle.

A flipchart may be used as a substitute blackboard. It has the advantage of being easily portable. One particular use of the flipchart is in group work. If small groups of learners are required to think about a particular topic and offer suggestions, then their ideas can be recorded on a flipchart which can then be presented to the whole group. The flipchart pages from all the groups can then be displayed together so that similarities and differences can be seen.

Nowadays, with the growth in popularity of the overhead projector and handouts, the blackboard is not used as much for presenting prepared information but rather is used for spontaneous clarification of points that derive from the interaction between teachers and learners. Information gained through 'brainstorming' could also be recorded in this way.

Medical equipment and models

Some of the most useful visual aids are examples of equipment used in everyday practice. Portable specimens such as aids to daily living, communication charts, splints, prostheses and inhalers, to name but a few, can be shown to the whole group and passed round for each member to handle. Therapists are in the ideal situation of having ready access to equipment such as this.

Models also have a place in the therapist's repertoire of aids. One example is a model of the spine, complete with spinal cord and issuing nerve roots, which is an invaluable adjunct to teaching the principles of safe lifting, while another is a functional model of the larynx, which can be used to clarify the exact position of the vocal cords. Models can be purchased from such companies as Adam, Rouilly London Ltd. and while involving an initial outlay, are well worth the expense in the long term.

A range of posters may also be purchased from the above company and can be displayed around the room either for learners to refer to during an appropriate activity or in their own time.

Conclusion

Audio-visual aids, when carefully selected, are invaluable learning resources, but if they are to be made then sufficient time must be set aside in order to produce material of a high quality. If they are scrappy, poorly designed or irrelevant, then it will reflect on therapists and their teaching commitment may be thrown into question.

Useful addresses

Graves Educational Resources
220 New London Road
Chelmsford
Essex
CM2 9BJ

Adam, Rouilly London Ltd.
Crown Quay Lane
Sittingbourne
Kent
MR10 3JG

Part Three

Ways of Teaching and Learning

6

The Lecture

It is not uncommon for therapists to be called upon to give lectures. They may be asked to do so after attending a course or conference, after working overseas, or completing some research, so that colleagues may benefit from the knowledge they have gained. The teaching of students and junior colleagues may be part of their job description, and at times they may be required to lecture those from other professions, such as nurses and doctors. We are all familiar with the lecture as a mode of instruction; Bligh (1980) points out that it is the most common teaching method used in universities throughout the world. Although times have changed, this is probably still true of many therapy courses and conferences today.

It is likely that the work therapists do with patients and clients gives them valuable preparation for lecturing, as it involves the skills of explaining and communicating. Some people are fortunate to have a natural flair for lecturing, but most find it daunting and difficult even when the learners are familiar. The ability to lecture is not an innate gift, however, but a skill which can be learned and improved upon with practice.

The skill of lecturing

Preparation

Brown and Atkins contend that, 'the essential skill of effective lecturing is preparation not presentation' (1988: 35). The actual *giving* of a lecture comes at the end of a long process of preparation.

When preparing a lecture it is important to realize that most people cannot listen attentively to someone speaking for more than about twenty minutes. Newble and Cannon (1991) point out that learners' concentration and performance during a lecture falls steadily after the first few minutes, reviving very slightly just before the end. Having a short rest or a change of activity increases arousal and attention with a subsequent improvement in motivation and learning. This is a gain which more than compensates for any loss of time. The therapist's performance will also be enhanced by taking short breaks.

In view of the average learner's short concentration span, it is generally better to give a number of 'lecturettes' interspersed with other activities and short rest periods, rather than one long lecture. The learners may, for example, be asked to discuss an issue in small groups, to practise a skill, to work out a problem or to read a short extract. Audio-visual aids, such as overhead projectors, films and slides, bring variety and interest to lectures as well as acting as prompts for lecturers. Any change of activity is likely to renew interest. Brown and Atkins state:

> It does not follow that because you have a lecture class for one hour you have to talk for the whole hour. By varying student activities throughout a lecture you can renew their attention, generate interest, provide opportunities for students to think and obtain some feedback on their understanding. (1988: 28)

(The use of audio-visual materials is discussed in chapter 5. Active learning during lectures is discussed in chapter 7.)

It is very important to keep the learners constantly in mind when planning a lecture. How much background knowledge do they have? What information do they need or want? Is the lecture taking place on a Friday afternoon when people will need extra stimulation? Does anyone have special learning needs? Teaching heterogeneous groups is particularly demanding. Before concentrating on the actual subject matter of the lecture, it is important to find out what resources will be available to you when the lecture is given.

Probably the most common error when delivering a lecture is to present too much material too quickly. This can be avoided by thinking carefully about what you want to say so that your preparation is directed. Rather than going into great detail on a subject, it is best to outline the main concepts and underlying principles, enabling learners to pursue the subject in greater depth if they wish. Gibbs et al. state that, 'Students' notes from lectures may often reveal their preoccupation with minutiae and factual detail at the expense of broad themes' (1988: 95). They contend that much can be learned about the effectiveness of lectures by looking at learners' notes.

Beard (1976) believes that the content of lectures should not be too abstract, but rather should contain illustrations and applications of relevance to the learners which can be linked with their previous experience. Efforts should be made, where appropriate, to link theory with practice.

Setting educational objectives

It may be helpful to formulate a list of objectives. This will focus therapists' thoughts and deter them from straying too far from the subject; it will also remind them of the learners' needs. Educational objectives specify what the therapist expects the learners to know or achieve by the end of the lecture, or series of lectures. If the lecture concerns the value of different eating utensils for people with severe rheumatoid arthritis, for example, one of the objectives may be formulated as follows:

> At the end of this lecture the learners should be able to choose appropriate eating utensils for people with severe rheumatoid arthritis affecting the hands.

(For further information on setting educational objectives, the reader is referred to chapter 4.)

Brainstorming

When the objectives have been worked out, the next step is to think about the content of the lecture in more detail. A brainstorming session, where all the ideas, theories and examples the therapist can think of on the topic are written down, is a good way to start. This can either be done alone or with a few colleagues. The therapist will probably already have a great deal of information on the topic, so the exercise is likely to be reassuring. The construction of a 'thought map' from the brainstorming session also helps to loosen up mental processes and encourage lateral thinking. An example of a thought map is shown in Figure 6.1. The lecture to be given is on clinical interviewing.

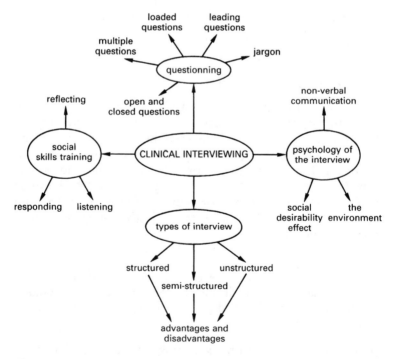

Figure 6.1 *A thought map*

Therapists may find that their knowledge of the topic is a little sparse in places and that they need to do some reading. At this stage they should also be looking out for suitable audio-visual materials, such as cartoons, jokes, films and anything else which they feel will enhance their teaching. The lecture will also be enlivened by relevant case studies and anecdotes from clinical experience.

Handouts

A decision therapists will need to make during their preparation is whether or not to provide the learners with a handout. Some teachers prepare handouts to relieve the learners of notetaking. There are differing views on the wisdom of this; notetaking certainly brings some activity to rather passive teaching methods like the lecture, but for some people it interferes with comprehension. In addition, notetaking is a skill in itself which many people do not possess. If handouts are given they should be short, summarizing the main points; if they are long and elaborate, the chances are they will not be read. Giving learners copies of complex diagrams can save a lot of time during lectures. (For further information on handouts, the reader is referred to chapter 5.)

Organizing your material

Having gathered together all the material, the next task is to organize it logically and coherently so that it is easily followed; information will not be transferred to long-term memory unless it is understood. The structure may consist of a simple list of topic areas to be covered, for example:

The shoulder region
Bones
Muscles
Joints
Nerves
Blood vessels
Lymph nodes

Alternatively it may consist of a comparison between two or more key concepts, for example:

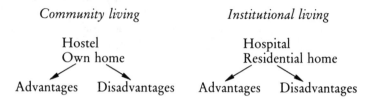

or there may be a central problem with a variety of solutions, for example:

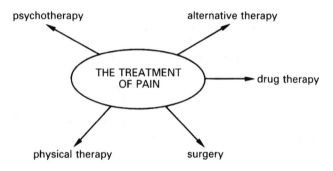

Figure 6.2 *Central problem with a variety of solutions*

The physical environment

Thought should be given to the room and the furniture in the room where the lecture will take place. If the learners are to form small discussion groups, for example, a lecture theatre with fixed furniture, or a very cramped room, would be unsuitable. Sometimes the physical environment is outside the therapist's control and compromises have to be made, but it is worth negotiating for the best possible venue. It is essential to know what sort of room and facilities will be available before giving the lecture.

Presentation

If a lecture is prepared with care it will almost certainly be a success, but there is more that can be done to ensure that it is. Many people find it beneficial to rehearse the lecture, either to themselves or to a few colleagues. This can help to build confidence and reduce anxiety.

Starting the lecture

At the start of the lecture, the therapist should let the learners know what the objectives are, and explain how the available time will be spent. There are many ways of giving a lecture and it often helps if teachers briefly state their own particular 'ground rules' so that learners know how to behave and are not inhibited or confused. For example, the therapist may like to assure them that they can interrupt to ask questions, that they can say if they do not understand, or that the contribution of their ideas and experiences is welcomed. If there is time, or if the therapist is giving a series of lectures, these ground rules may be negotiated with the learners.

On entering the room, therapists should give themselves and the learners a minute or two to sort out notes and stationery, and to become orientated. Feelings of nervousness can be allayed by directing attention to the needs of the learners. The therapist should speak a little slower than normal and ensure that everything said can be heard clearly.

Self-presentation

It is vital that therapists convey enthusiasm and interest for their subject if they are to motivate and stimulate others. This is partly achieved by their non-verbal communication – facial expression, tone of voice, posture and so on. Non-verbal communication conveying enthusiasm, interest and friendship will help gain rapport with the learners. It is very difficult to display behaviour of this type if these emotions are not genuinely felt. Sensitivity to the learners' non-verbal communication is also important. Curzon states that:

A lecture is dependent for its success – to a marked degree – on the personality and communication skills of the lecturer. He is the sole focus of attention for much of the lecture period; his style of delivery can result in acceptance and assimilation, or rejection, of the lecture content. (1990: 279)

Therapists should avoid excessive writing on the blackboard as this can give the impression of being more interested in the subject matter than the learners, as well as wasting time. If a large amount of material is to be displayed, it is best to prepare it in advance. Using an overhead projector, rather than a blackboard, will mean that the therapist does not have to face away from the learners.

Attending to notes excessively can also lead to lack of rapport. It is best if therapists are familiar enough with the subject matter, and sufficiently confident, that they are able to manage without a detailed record. Many teachers simply bring a list of key words and phrases to the lecture, often written on small cards, others use their visual teaching aids to prompt them. Lecturing without reference to detailed notes only comes with time and practice; therapists new to the task may prefer to keep a full set of notes nearby for reassurance and reference if necessary. Therapists should not worry if they need to use their notes, or they lose their place, or if their mind goes blank occasionally; this happens to all teachers however experienced they are. Learners do not expect perfection from teachers.

It is often said that it helps to be a good actor, to tell jokes and funny stories to hold the attention of the learners. Beard (1976), however, warns that there is the danger that the showman-type teacher may be so impressive that the learners will fail to think for themselves or criticize what has been said. Curzon (1990) warns that jokes and extraneous remarks may be remembered more clearly than the main points of the lecture, and interest is unlikely to last if the lecture is deficient in substance (Brown and Atkins, 1988). Newble and Cannon believe that 'the attention of the students ought to be engaged by the subject of the lecture rather than the personality of the lecturer' (1991: 8). The humorous teacher does, however, have a valuable gift, provided it does not detract from the main purpose of the lecture.

Questioning

One way to achieve learner participation in lectures is to ask questions. This must, however, be done carefully if it is to be successful. Newble and Cannon (1991) point out that the main emotion associated with questioning is fear, which is not conducive to learning; we are probably all aware of the truth of this from our own experience. As a general rule it is best if therapists ask questions of the whole group, unless they are aware that a particular person has a great deal of knowledge on the topic to offer.

Asking learners if they have any questions during the lecture or at the end of the lecture is not always very successful. Gibbs et al. (1988) suggest that this is because learners are given insufficient time to think, that they are too inhibited, or that they are so busy writing during the lecture that they have little opportunity to formulate questions. There may also be an unspoken ground rule that the lecture must be 'got through' at all costs, and that if questions are asked the therapist will rush, or the coffee break will be shortened or missed. Group norms may also inhibit questioning, and learners who go against them may be resented by their fellow learners and the therapist. Learners should be given time to formulate their questions, and questioning should be made an integral part of the lecture for which adequate time is given. Therapists should not worry if they do not know the answer to all the learners' questions; learners do not expect those who teach them to be superhuman.

Structuring the lecture

Gibbs et al. believe that learners should be made aware of the structure of lectures, they state:

> it is the structure which students often have most difficulty in perceiving, and their notes often reveal only an undifferen-

tiated linear sequence of contents. If you can identify the key structuring elements of your lecture and give the information to your students, you can be very helpful to them. (1988: 63)

It is most useful to learners if teachers present them with the key points, while avoiding too much detail. These points, as well as the overall structure of the lecture, can be displayed on a blackboard or overhead projector so that the learners keep them in mind. When starting to study a new subject area it is very difficult to distinguish key points from those which are less central or important, so they need to be emphasized. Newble and Cannon (1991) suggest the following lecture format which can, of course, be adapted by therapists to suit their individual purposes:

Present first key point
  Develop the ideas
  Give examples
  Reiterate the first key point

Present second key point
  Develop the ideas
  Give examples
  Reiterate the first and second key points

Present third key point
  Develop the ideas
  Give examples
  Reiterate first, second and third key points

Summary and conclusion

It can be seen that there is a certain amount of repetition in the above plan. This is helpful as it not only stresses the main points, but serves to aid memory and understanding.

The opening and conclusion of the lecture are very important; what is said first and last are likely to be remembered best. The opening, in particular, should arouse interest, and the conclusion should draw together and reiterate the main themes and direct the learners to additional sources of information. It can be helpful to give learners a few minutes at the end of the lecture to read through their notes, highlighting any points they do not fully understand so that they can work on them later, or bring them to a subsequent tutorial. The conclusion of the lecture is a good time to make explicit links between this lecture and the last, this lecture and the one to come, and this aspect of the course with other aspects. The importance of making these connections should be stressed, and work may be set to clarify and consolidate them.

The reference list provided should be clear and realistically short; it can be very daunting and stressful to be presented with a long list. It will help learners if they are given information regarding the most important references. The list should not necessarily be confined to books and journals; it may include, for example, films, radio programmes, or the unpublished literature of an organization. (For information on the preparation and presentation of conference papers, the reader is referred to chapter 16.)

Disadvantages of the lecture

We can probably all recall dreary lectures and lecturers, those who went too fast or whose lectures had no structure, those who were so wrapped up in the topic that they seemed oblivious to the needs of the learners, those from whom it was impossible to take decent notes and those who seemed thoroughly disenchanted with the subject matter. Indeed, there have been many criticisms of lecturers and the lecture as a teaching method.

The problem with lectures is that, from the learners' point of view, they are passive. This may suit some people as listening is less demanding and threatening than participation. Rogers believes that, 'Lectures and demonstrations notoriously allow students to daydream, do crosswords, write letters or even to gossip in whispers' (1989: 118). Beard (1976) points out that passive learning is less effective than active learning, and Rogers states 'far too many lecturers and demonstrators assume that their listeners have some hole in the head into which information can conveniently be poured'

(1989: 124). In many ways the lecture is easier and less stressful for teachers too, as it can be planned in advance and structured in such a way that there is little opportunity for learners to disagree or to challenge.

Time to raise questions and discuss issues is usually very limited in lectures and, in any event, many people are too intimidated to speak up. Curzon (1990) believes that the lecture is an autocratic teaching method; the learners are exposed to one person's perspective which, even with care, is bound to be biased. In addition lectures put a tremendous strain on the short term memory, and feedback to teachers, to allow them to adjust to learners, is very limited. This makes evaluation of lectures important.

Advantages of the lecture

Lecturing as a teaching method is not all bad, however. The lecture can be a successful method for introducing a topic and providing learners with a framework for independent study. Although the method does not appear ideal for bringing about attitude change, or teaching learners how to think or solve problems, it is at least as good as other methods for imparting information (Bligh, 1971; Hartley, 1984). Lectures are also useful for introducing subject matter which has yet to be published, and for combining knowledge from a large number of sources into a digestible whole.

Lectures are economical in terms of both time and money as large groups of people can be reached with minimal resources; no doubt this is one reason why the lecture remains so popular. If the aims of the teaching are not fulfilled by using the lecture, however, this will cease to be an advantage.

Conclusion

The lecture is not a perfect teaching method, for no one method is. It can, however, be very useful to therapists engaged in teaching, especially when learner participation is included in its structure (see chapter 7). As Curzon states, 'Carefully prepared, well timed and skilfully delivered with "a touch of colour, a hint of wonder" the lecture can be a powerful and stimulating mode of communication and instruction' (1990: 284).

7

Active Learning During Lectures

In chapter 6 on the lecture, it was pointed out that most people cannot listen attentively to someone speaking for more than about twenty minutes, and that the performance of learners in lectures can be greatly enhanced by varying the learning activities. Gibbs et al. state:

> if relatively little is achieved after twenty minutes it seems sensible to stop and do something else. Once one has reconceptualised lectures as much shorter events, all sorts of possibilities open up. (1988: 101)

Even if therapists are only teaching for an hour or two, there are many activities which can be incorporated into their lectures. These will help to hold the interest of the learners and will encourage participation. This is particularly important when teaching large groups where many people feel inhibited. In a lecture on back care and lifting, for example, the therapist could divide the learners into small groups and ask each to decide how back injuries could best be avoided in their line of work. Provided the subject area touches people's everyday lives, most of the knowledge will be contained within the group.

An added advantage of participation is that learners are frequently surprised by the extent of their own knowledge, and often gain confidence as a result. It also encourages them to learn from each other. It is important that therapists do not feel redundant or useless if this is the case, for education is basically a process of facilitation rather than one of bombarding learners with facts.

Traditionally learners discuss the content of lectures, and any problems they have with them, in tutorials which take place some time later; it is here too that ideas are often applied to practice. Gibbs et al. (1988) believe, however, that ideas should be applied immediately and that discussion may be of a higher quality in groups without a teacher. Instead of tutorials, they believe that discussion and problem solving should take place during lectures.

In this chapter a variety of activities which can be used in lectures will be discussed. Most of the suggestions are also appropriate for use in large discussion groups.

Small group activities

During the lecture it can be useful to divide the learners into small groups. This has the advantage that those who tend not to participate in a larger context may contribute their ideas and gain confidence. Learners can also test ideas on a few of their peers before presenting them to the whole group. Below are some examples of small group work.

Buzz groups

These groups are so called because of the buzz of activity which emanates from them. Learners are divided into small groups of three or four and are asked to discuss a topic, usually for about ten minutes. The learners are generally left alone, although the therapist may circulate and offer help if required. An occupational therapist giving a lecture on Parkinson's disease, for example, may divide the learners into buzz groups to discuss treatment strategies, or a physiotherapist giving a lecture on community care in terminal illness, may ask learners to compare the community approach with hospital-based treatment.

After the discussion, a spokesperson from each buzz group may share its conclusions with the whole group. The therapist, or another learner, should summarize the main points which are raised on a blackboard, flipchart or overhead projector, for later discussion or for use in subsequent lectures. The therapist needs to have a repertoire of buzz group activities so that they do not become boring.

Problem-solving or syndicate groups

A 'problem-solving' or 'syndicate' group is one in which a small group of learners are asked to pool their knowledge to solve a particular problem. An occupational therapist working on a spinal injuries unit may ask the learners to analyse the degree of impairment expected following trauma at various levels of the spinal cord; or a speech and language therapist working in a stroke unit may ask the learners to devise treatment strategies on the basis of various signs and symptoms. Having solved the problem, a spokesperson from each syndicate group may report back to the whole group, or the material may be used for later discussion or incorporation into subsequent lectures.

Pyramid groups (snowball groups)

With this method the learners start by working on their own or in pairs to solve a problem or collect ideas on a topic. Each pair of learners then compares its ideas with another pair of learners, each quartet with another quartet and so on; the pyramids can terminate at any size, usually at four or eight people.

A different task may be set for each stage, for example a therapist may ask the pairs of learners to consider what causes drug addiction, the quartets may be asked to consider possible solutions to the situation, and the groups of eight may be asked to suggest ways of implementing the solutions. One person from each pyramid group should be given the task of reporting back to the whole group.

Brainstorming

In this activity learners are asked to think of as many ideas on a given issue, or as many solutions to a given problem, as possible; they may work alone, in pairs, or in small groups. The object of brainstorming is to generate ideas rather than evaluate them, it provides a diversity of viewpoints and encourages divergent thinking. The ideas that emerge can be shared with the whole group, and may be summarized by the therapist or one of the learners for further discussion or future use.

Peer tutoring

Pairs of learners can be asked to teach each other. After the therapist has lectured for fifteen minutes, for example, the learners may be asked to seek help from their immediate neighbours with any aspect of the lecture they did not fully understand; their roles can then be reversed. Peer tutoring encourages learners to share their knowledge and provides them with the opportunity to teach others which, in itself, is an excellent way to consolidate new information.

Managing small groups

Very specific instructions need to be given if small group activities are to work well; the learners must know precisely what is required of them or muddle will ensue. The timing must also be correct, it is frustrating and demotivating to be interrupted before the work is complete, yet if too much time is given boredom may develop. A certain amount of time pressure can inspire good group work, though too little time can trivialize the tasks undertaken. Flexibility on the part of the therapist is needed, if learners are engrossed in discussion, and are obviously benefiting from it, the planned time period may be extended.

Furniture should be arranged appropriately to enhance discussion, learners should sit so that they can see each other clearly. Equipment should be available to enable them to work efficiently and comfortably, they should not, for example, be expected to write without an adequate surface. Learners may need to go to different rooms, or even outside the building, to carry out specific assignments; they may, for example, need to visit the library to solve a particular problem.

Independent work in lectures

Lectures may be broken up by giving learners short pieces of work to undertake on their own. They may, for example, be asked to solve a problem, draw a graph, label a blank diagram, design an experiment, or simply to think.

Reading

Learners may be asked to reach a conclusion on a given issue after reading a short extract or article during the lecture. A short discussion may then follow, or the learners may be asked to write their conclusions on cards which the therapist or the learners can collate and use as the basis for the next session. Some people may be reluctant to set learners reading tasks in lecture time but Gibbs et al. believe that:

> If a good text exists, then reading is far better than listening to a lecture. You need to have some fairly sound reason for wanting to lecture at all with such competition . . . Lecturing is perhaps best left for those occasions for which no suitable text can be found. (1988: 129)

Reading can also be used to give learners practice in extracting relevant material from text.

Time to think

It is quite unnecessary for lectures to be filled entirely with frantic activity, in fact it is very valuable to give learners a few minutes to think quietly at regular points throughout the lecture. The task of taking notes often means that learners have little time to think while the lecture is in progress. The therapist could, for example, give learners a few minutes to formulate questions before asking them, or time to think about a difficult point that has just been explained before moving on to the next.

The mini-presentation

Learners can be asked to present a topic to the whole group, lasting perhaps ten or fifteen minutes. They may be asked to do so within the context of a lecture, although it is less threatening for inexperienced people if the group is small. The topic of the presentation may be the learner's own work, for example a project or a piece of research. In this situation the learner is in charge and is required to prepare the presentation, using audio-visual aids, and to manage any questions or discussion which follows.

The project or research does not need to be complete in order to undertake this task; the learner may be in the middle of it, or even at the planning stage, but will none the less gain a great deal by listening and responding to the comments, questions and criticisms of others. An alternative strategy is for a number of learners to conduct a longer presentation, each being responsible for an aspect of it.

This method is suitable if the therapist has an on-going teaching commitment to the same group of people. A head occupational therapist, for example, may require each member of staff to present an interesting aspect of work for others to discuss. Alternatively a senior physiotherapist, perhaps involved in running a course on orthopaedic medicine, may require each course participant to carry out a mini-presentation based on a project or a case study of his or her own work in that area.

The mini-presentation provides learners with practice in presenting material clearly, which is a skill many will need in their professional lives. In order to present the material well and to cope with any questions and queries which are raised, learners will need to clarify their own thoughts and understand the subject matter in depth. Poor presentations can very quickly lead to boredom and inattentiveness on the part of the audience; the therapist should advise and help learners to plan their presentation, if necessary, and be ready to assist at any time if serious difficulties arise.

Testing

Testing can be used at any point during the lecture, for example a short test may be given at the beginning to aid memorization and review the work of previous lectures. Warning of the test may or may not be given, and it may be self-marked, or marked by the therapist or a fellow learner. Short tests or quizzes can also be given during the lecture or at the end as a way of reviewing and consolidating knowledge. They provide feedback to both therapist and learners so that areas of difficulty can be addressed.

A disadvantage of tests is that they tend to create anxiety. This should be avoided as far as possible by presenting them in a light hearted way as an aid to learning. Tests can, of course, be carried out in pairs or in small groups rather than individually.

Observation

Observation is a passive way to learn and should therefore be used with caution during a lecture which is, in itself, a passive method. Nevertheless, along with the more dynamic activities, it can be useful and does have a place. Therapists may, for example, show the learners a video extract or ask them to listen to an audio-tape. Alternatively, they may demonstrate a treatment technique or present a patient. It is very important that all the learners can see and hear exactly what is happening, though this can be difficult to achieve in a large lecture room. Showing a video of a treatment technique may be more successful than a live performance.

Reviewing

review is one of the most powerful and easily demonstrated devices for improving learning from lectures. And the sooner after the end of the lecture the review takes place the greater is its effect (Gibbs et al. 1988: 39)

It is well worth giving the learners a little time at the end of the lecture to review what they have learned. They may simply be given a few minutes to read through what they have written, or they may be asked to explain various aspects of the lecture material to a fellow learner, from memory or using their notes. Another way of reviewing the lecture is to ask the learners to write down what they consider to be the three most important points which were raised. These can be compared and any differences of opinion can be discussed.

Conclusion

Many therapists, particularly those over the age of thirty-five, are likely to have been fed an educational diet of 'talk and chalk'. Although the lecture as a teaching method does have its place, it is likely to be more successful if some of the activities suggested above are incorporated into it. There are no hard and fast rules; what the therapist should try to achieve is a high level of enthusiasm, motivation and interest, with plenty of opportunities for active learning.

8

Small Group Teaching

When asked to teach, many therapists may, understandably, be tempted to lecture to large groups of people, in order to save themselves time. However, learners, be they undergraduates, colleagues or people from other professions, are likely to assimilate more if they are taught in a small group setting. In this situation there is greater opportunity for participation and for therapists to offer individuals immediate feedback and help when required. Seminars and tutorials are useful methods for achieving these aims.

Seminars

The seminar is a small group teaching method where, ideally, the number of learners should not exceed ten. A learner, or possibly two learners, are asked to present a paper to the rest of the group which is then discussed. If the seminar is part of a series, a list of topics and dates may be offered to the learners from which they can choose.

Curzon states that, 'The seminar appears to be appropriate as a mode of instruction when the level of attainment of the group is relatively high and the subject matter lends itself to analytical treatment' (1990: 292). Presenters will gain useful experience in various teaching and communication skills, and their ability to formulate and sustain an argument will be tested to the full. They will also need to understand the subject matter in depth in order to cope with the discussion and questioning which follows the presentation.

The learners leading the seminar should be encouraged to make it as interesting as possible by using audio-visual aids and facilitating group participation. They may also prepare a handout and reference list. Although the learners may require some advice, the therapist should resist all temptation to take over unless real difficulties arise. If the learner becomes seriously confused or flustered during the presentation, for example, the therapist may offer reassurance and encouragement, clarify the arguments, or reiterate the point which has been reached.

Following the presentation, the learners and the therapist are free to ask questions and to analyse the paper. It is important that the seating is arranged to facilitate discussion. The presenters should then be given feedback. One way of achieving this is to ask them to state one positive and one negative aspect of their own performance; each member of the group can then be asked to do the same. Few presentations are wholly bad and whenever possible it is important to balance criticism with praise so as to avoid discouragement. It is good practice for the therapist to summarize the main points at the end of the seminar, and to link them with past and future learning.

A major problem with seminars is poor understanding of the material by those not involved in the presentation. Brown and Atkins (1988) believe that the seminar is prone to degenerate into a conversation between the presenter and the teacher. Lack of presentation skill can also be a problem as the audience is likely to lose interest if it falls below a certain level. These problems can be overcome by careful planning and preparation on the part of the therapist and presenters. In order that all the learners can comprehend the seminar material, for example, it is useful if a summary is prepared for distribution in advance, though this will be unnecessary if the seminar is linked to a previous lecture or discussion.

The seminar is of limited value if therapists have a 'one-off' hour or two to spend teaching, but can be very useful as part of a longer course, or where they have ongoing contact with learners. It may, for example, be possible for clinical therapists to arrange seminars to consolidate the clinical learning of undergraduate students. It is a method which involves considerable work from learners so sufficient time must be given for preparation.

Tutorials

Tutorials involve the teaching of one learner or a group of learners ideally not exceeding five (Brown and Atkins, 1988). It is a teaching method associated with the older universities and, if used frequently, requires a high learner–teacher ratio. The purpose of tutorials varies; learners may be asked to present and discuss their essays, or to ask questions concerning previous work. They may be required to discuss progress with projects, research or case presentations. Alternatively tutorials can be used for teaching and learning practical skills. They are a means of encouraging learners to work together and to learn from each other, and provide teachers with the opportunity to give help to individuals.

Although the number of learners in tutorials is small, they can still be separated into sub-groups or asked to work independently for a time. A group of eight could be broken into pairs with each pair being asked to consider a particular aspect of a problem. When considering the role of day hospitals, for example, one pair could be asked to concentrate on the medical aspects, another on the social aspects, a third on the psychological aspects, and a fourth on the managerial aspects. Brainstorming and buzz groups can also be used in tutorials (see chapter 7). It is a good idea to alter the composition of the sub-groups from time to time to enable learners to work with different people so as to encourage diverse perspectives and experiences.

It is perfectly legitimate to use audio-visual aids and other teaching materials in tutorials. Habeshaw et al. (1988) believe that visual aids, such as the blackboard or overhead projector, are sometimes avoided as teachers feel their use is too authoritarian in a setting designed to be relatively informal. This can, however, be overcome by asking a learner to do the writing. Handouts are also useful as a way of summarizing the main points of the tutorial, as it is difficult to take coherent notes during informal discussion. The handouts can be dynamic where, for example, the learners are asked to label a diagram or answer a series of questions. Learners can also be asked to bring material to the tutorial; for example, if the tutorial concerns community care, they may be asked to bring newspaper and magazine cuttings highlighting different viewpoints on the topic.

The close-knit nature of tutorial groups means they can easily degenerate into social events; this should not be totally avoided, as a friendly, sociable atmosphere facilitates learning and discussion. It does, however, need to be managed carefully if the original aims of the tutorial are to be met. Tutorials can be successful when teachers are absent. The therapist may, for example, decide to attend one tutorial in three, or simply to be available if learners need help. Habeshaw et al. (1988) believe that tutorials without teachers are more successful if they are started early in the course, before learners become passive and dependent.

Therapists can use tutorials to good effect. The senior therapist, for example, may use the method to teach a small group of junior colleagues a manual skill, or to discuss the treatment of a particular patient or client. Therapists are increasingly expected to carry out projects and research as part of their clinical role, and the tutorial is an ideal way of highlighting and discussing difficulties and achievements either on a one-to-one basis or in a small group.

Running small groups

Introductions

When a group of people meet for the first time for a seminar or a tutorial, it is important to spend some time on introductions. This helps learners to relate to each other and to feel relaxed. The therapist may simply ask the learners to introduce themselves to the whole group, explaining what they hope to achieve from the meetings, or why they have come. Alternately they can be separated into pairs and asked to talk about themselves for a few minutes. The members of each pair can then introduce each other to the whole group. Another way of disposing of barriers quickly is to break the learners into groups of three or four and ask them to discover three things they have in common, this can then be shared with the whole group.

It is very important that group members quickly learn each other's names. This can be facilitated by asking them to state their names before speaking for the first meeting or two; name badges will also help. Alternatively each learner may be asked to go around the circle attempting to remember everyone's name. This can then be repeated with the learners sitting in different places. The fun of these activities can, in itself, help to break down barriers.

Drawing up a contract

There are many 'ground rules' operating in educational settings which usually remain unspoken, but which can greatly influence the behaviour of both learners and teachers. These unspoken rules are often authoritarian in nature, such as not interrupting teachers when they are speaking, or allowing teachers to take full responsibility for organizing the group. Learners may, for example, be reluctant to invite another learner to speak, or to begin a discussion in the absence of the therapist. This behaviour results from habit as well as a fear of violating the conventional roles of 'student' and 'teacher'. It is well worth discussing and negotiating appropriate ground rules at the onset of a session or a course; those which maximize learner participation and control should generally be encouraged.

Learner participation

In the small-group setting, responsibility can be shifted from the therapist to the learners. For example, during a discussion, one learner could act as chairperson, another as time-keeper, and a third as scribe. Learners should be encouraged to listen to each other and to ask each other questions. Self-disclosure by the therapist, concerning lack of knowledge or difficulty with a task, can be very reassuring as it makes ignorance and uncertainty acceptable.

Learners should take responsibility for the climate of the group; if something goes wrong they should be encouraged to discuss it openly and sort it out. It may be that someone is dominating the group, that a clique has developed, or that the work is unevenly spread. The problem may, of course, concern the therapist who, as an equal member of the group, must also be open to criticism.

Conclusion

The seminar and tutorial are teaching methods which provide learners with opportunities to participate actively and for teachers to offer individual help. They are particularly valuable methods to therapists who work with small groups of students or colleagues for extended periods of time.

9

The Discussion Group

The purpose of a discussion group is usually the collective exploration and 'public evaluation' of ideas (Curzon, 1990: 287)

When called upon to teach, the first method that may spring to mind is the lecture, but in some circumstances a discussion may be of greater value. Group discussion is an active, democratic teaching method where each participant has the right to contribute ideas, and in which the teacher does not dominate. The members of the group pool their knowledge and learn from each other.

Discussion is a particularly useful method for exploring complex, multifaceted issues. By considering the interpretations and ideas of others, individual learners are provided with a wider perspective. Beard (1976) believes that, rather than imparting new facts, the discussion is an ideal way of enabling learners to rearrange and reassess their ideas.

Preparing a discussion group

Although the therapist should generally take a 'back seat' in discussions, this does not mean that no preparation is required. Preparing for a discussion is, in fact, more demanding than lecture preparation, because the therapist has less control over proceedings and cannot fully anticipate where the discussion will lead. Therapists who decide to use this method must have a sound grasp of the subject matter themselves.

Before deciding to use group discussion, it is important to clarify why it is the most appropriate method, and what its function will be; is it to consolidate previous learning, to explore a familiar issue in more depth, or to give learners the opportunity to expose their ideas to scrutiny? Writing a list of objectives will help to focus the mind on this. Objectives specify what the teacher expects the learners to be able to do at the end of the discussion. For example, if it concerns the integration of adults with severe learning disabilities into the community, one of the objectives may be: 'at the end of the discussion the learners should be able to identify a range of opinions both for and against the integration of adults with severe learning disabilities into the community.' The purpose of the discussion must be made clear to the learners before it begins. (For further information on learning objectives, the reader is referred to chapter 4.)

Detailed notes are not necessary when planning a discussion, but an outline plan should be made. Curzon (1990) suggests prepared questions to provoke thought or to move the discussion on. The therapist can prepare audio-visual materials, although it may be unnecessary or inappropriate to use them. The therapist should also decide in advance what work the learners will be given to consolidate what they have learned, and how the new knowledge relates to what they have covered before and what will be learned in the future.

The arrangement of furniture has been shown to have an enormous impact on communication (Adler and Rodman, 1991). Learners should be able to see each other clearly, and therapists should not stand out in any way, for example by interposing desks between themselves and the learners, or taking a particularly prominent position. Seating can be arranged to bring about certain effects, for example two persistent talkers could sit adjacent, rather than opposite, each other to reduce their output, or a 'talker' could sit opposite someone who tends to remain silent to encourage that person to participate (Brown and Atkins, 1988).

The overall composition of the group may also need some thought. Stevenson and Parsloe state that 'being in a minority, and especially a minority of one, is not an empowering experience, and those who construct learning groups need to

consider membership in terms of race, gender and disability'
(1993: 57).

Running a discussion group

> On opening up discussion you are offering the class some-
> thing free, floating and unpredictable . . . It is only when your
> students can see that you are genuinely offering them oppor-
> tunities to speculate, think and interpret that new ideas will
> flourish. (Rogers 1989: 180)

Running a discussion group well is not an easy task but is one
which can be learned and improved upon with practice. The
first part of the discussion is usually the most difficult to
manage as it can be rather stilted. This can be avoided by
ensuring that the learners are well prepared; it may, for
example, follow a lecture, some practical work or a reading
assignment. Marshall and Rowland (1983) go as far as to say
that if students are unprepared for the discussion it is
probably better cancelled. Another approach is to precede the
discussion with a stimulating activity designed to provoke
debate, such as watching a short video extract, taking part in
some role play, or listening to an audiotape.

The role of the therapist is basically that of informal
chairperson. Rather than controlling the content of the
discussion, the therapist should listen carefully to what the
learners are saying, allow people who want to speak to do so,
provide necessary resources, and protect minority views. It
may be appropriate for the therapist to clarify issues at
various points in the discussion and to bring the learners back
to the topic if they stray too far from it. Therapists should be
flexible enough to abandon their plans; if, for example, the
discussion is lively and the learners are absorbed, it may be
unnecessary, and indeed disruptive, to use prepared materials,
or to insist that every aspect of the topic is explored.

Bligh (1976) suggests that teachers should not answer
questions which could be answered by a learner, that they
should not state their own opinions rigidly, and that they

should not correct or reject the first contributions made. However, Curzon (1990) believes that faulty reasoning and circular arguments should be remedied, that obscure statements should be clarified, and that sweeping generalizations should be examined. He believes that if the group has insufficient knowledge the discussion is likely to be 'little more than the ritual exchange of loose thinking' (1990: 387). Similarly Brown and Atkins believe that, 'It is relatively easy to have a vague meandering discussion, it is much more difficult for students to discuss coherently, to question and to think' (1988: 50). Janis (1972) found that the conclusions reached by groups were often wrong, especially if the groups were cohesive and conforming. He referred to the processes leading to this as 'groupthink'.

Findings such as these emphasize the need for careful planning; the group must have a constant flow of information and ideas, it is always a mistake to regard the activity as a time filler or a 'soft option'. Many of the small group techniques described in chapter 7 are appropriate for use in discussion groups. Learners may, on occasions, be asked to discuss a question with their immediate neighbour, they may be divided into 'buzz groups' to work out a problem, or engage in a brainstorming session to generate ideas before the discussion begins.

Disruptive behaviour on the part of learners cannot be disregarded; it is relatively easy in a lecture theatre to ignore a whispering couple in the back row, or someone who has fallen asleep or is reading a magazine, but in the context of a discussion group this behaviour must be confronted or it will adversely affect the group's functioning. Newble and Cannon (1991) advise that if there is a problem with the group it should be raised with the learners and that the adoption of an authoritarian style by the teacher is likely to be counterproductive. Thus, as well as ensuring that the work of the group is fulfilled, a favourable group atmosphere must be maintained; Newble and Cannon (1991) believe that the maintenance of a good climate for discussion is the responsibility of the learners as well as the teacher, and Marshall and Rowland state 'The success of a discussion group depends largely on whether everyone takes responsibility for how the group operates and whether everyone feels free to contribute fully' (1983: 123).

Learners considered to talk too much can usually be politely controlled, although this is by no means easy, especially as talkative people are often enthusiastic and valuable group members. Changing the seating may help, as may asking open questions such as 'What does anyone else think?' or 'Does anyone disagree?' which will direct the discussion to other people and other issues. Habeshaw et al. (1988) suggest that learners should rate themselves as high or low contributors and that the two groups should work separately at least some of the time. Some learners may remain silent. Silence is very difficult to interpret; it may signify disapproval of what is being said, but alternatively it can indicate shyness, laziness, fear of showing ignorance, or a preference to listen. Teachers are often afraid of silence and tend to intervene too soon with an opinion or idea of their own before learners have had sufficient time to think. It is unfortunate that infrequent talkers tend to be ignored and that their contributions are undervalued unless they get the support of a talkative member (Klein, 1985). Marshall and Rowland (1983) believe that people who rarely talk need encouragement; sometimes quiet members can be induced to talk by appealing to some special knowledge they possess and verbal and non-verbal reward when they do participate may also increase their output. Although teachers tend to get worried by silent learners, Rogers (1989) points out that there is no evidence that they learn less.

On occasions discussion can develop into heated argument. Although lively debate is to be encouraged, it is the role of the therapist to prevent arguments developing, as people will no longer be exchanging ideas or learning from each other; instead the discussion can turn into 'a battle where one side has to concede defeat and lose face' (Rogers 1989: 188). There is a place for exerting authority when arguments develop, though the line between a heated debate and an argument is fine and therapists, for fear of matters getting out of hand, may exercise control too soon. It may be possible to dissipate tension with a joke, by providing evidence on some issue, or asking another learner to contribute; occasionally it may be necessary to stop the argument altogether and remind the group of the task in hand.

It will not be uncommon for some learners to be as skilful, or more skilful, than the teacher in controlling both argument and talkative or disruptive learners.

A successful discussion is often very difficult to close. This should be done by summarizing the main issues and linking them to past and future work. If the discussion has been worthwhile it will no doubt continue over the coffee or lunch break.

Advantages of the discussion group

The discussion group provides a democratic, permissive and collaborative method which enhances higher level intellectual skills, facilitates social interaction, helps learners gain confidence and communication skills, provides the therapist with feedback regarding learners' knowledge, and consolidates material previously learned. Beard (1976) points out that active learning is more effective than passive learning.

Discussion groups frequently fail to reach these ideals, however. Perhaps the main reason for this is the difficulty teachers experience in taking a 'back seat', in allowing learners to participate freely, and in tolerating a certain degree of 'raggedness'. They may guide the discussion in subtle, or not-so-subtle ways, and reward learners, verbally or non-verbally, for supporting the teacher's views. Rogers states:

> Classroom discussions, closely analysed, will often reveal how frequently teachers capitalise on their traditional authority and on the humble feelings of their students. As a result many discussions in adult education and training are far from free or equal, because tutors, often quite unconsciously, guide, manipulate and dominate proceedings. (1989: 176)

The discussion is a valuable teaching method for changing attitudes. According to Beard (1976), attitude change is facilitated by exposure to different points of view, from constructive criticism from other learners, and from some withdrawal of the teacher's authority. Even if attitudes are not changed it may help learners to become more tolerant of different viewpoints and perspectives (Curzon 1990).

Therapists, in their teaching role, may aim to change both attitudes and behaviour. For example, they may wish to persuade carers to alter their lifting techniques in order to protect themselves from back injury, or to convince colleagues that a certain treatment technique is worthwhile. Discussion is likely to be more successful than a lecture in fulfilling these aims.

Disadvantages of the discussion groups

There are many difficulties which arise in group discussion which can readily be understood in terms of group dynamics (Douglas, 1983; Brown, 1988). Learners may lack the courage to talk when in a group or may be overwhelmed by the attentiveness of others when they do (Rogers 1989). Some people in the group may remain silent while others may talk excessively and dominate the proceedings, the group may split into cliques, and there may even be overt or covert hostility. A further problem with any group is the tendency of people to conform.

A further disadvantage of group discussion is the attitude of some learners to it. People who want to be passive, or are used to a more conventional style of teaching, may object to the discussion method, at least initially. It may seem to them inconclusive, or they may feel that the therapist is not fulfilling the required role. Brown and Atkins (1988) suggest that an initial session with the learners, where the purpose of the method is explored, may be helpful in overcoming this type of resistance.

On a more practical note, the group discussion is expensive in terms of both time and staff resources. This is because the number of learners is low, and the amount of material covered is often small when compared with methods like the lecture.

Debates

A debate is a rather formal type of discussion where two sides of an argument are juxtaposed and judged. A debate on any controversial topic can be staged. This is achieved by asking one or more learner to gather and present information in support of a given motion, and for one or more learner to gather and present information against the motion. The debate may, for example, concern the effectiveness of physiotherapy in the relief of pain. In this case one learner would present evidence supporting the motion that physiotherapy is effective, and another learner would present evidence which suggests it is not. Each learner would be given fifteen to twenty minutes to speak, after which the other learners and the therapist would be free to ask questions and express opinions. Finally a vote for or against the motion would be taken.

The method demands considerable knowledge of a complex issue for those involved in presenting the evidence; they must be able to support and justify their arguments when challenged by the audience. The body of the hall should also know in advance what the topic of debate is to be. A disadvantage of the method is that the bulk of the work falls on just a few learners, though this may not matter in the context of a course or a series of teaching sessions. Those presenting the evidence are certain to learn a great deal.

Conclusion

The discussion and the debate are useful and valuable teaching methods and ones which can be used by any therapist who is asked to teach, whether to colleagues, patients, or the general public. The enormous wealth of information and experience which most adults possess should never be underestimated, and the discussion provides an ideal way of drawing it out. Although therapists may have had more opportunity than other group members to study in detail the topic in question, it is usually the case that they will learn something, often a great deal, themselves. This new knowledge can then be incorporated into future discussions, enhancing their quality.

The therapist who runs a discussion group or a debate among colleagues, students or clients, will be providing them with many learning opportunities and may find that, although these methods are time-consuming, the learners assimilate and remember more than they would by more passive or conventional means.

10

Role Play and Simulation

Role play

> Role playing in the classroom is one of the best ways to bring learning close to real life – and to make it fun. (Weiner and Bower, 1982: 14)

In role-play exercises, learners act out roles without a specific script although they are usually given information about the characters they are to play, and the situations they are in. Dickson et al. (1991) point out that role play can be structured, semi-structured or unstructured. In structured role play, the situation and the characters to be played are very precisely specified. In unstructured role play, on the other hand, learners are asked to improvise. The semi-structured approach lies between these two extremes. The roles may be written by the therapist or the learners, or the materials may have already been produced commercially.

Role play can be used to change behaviour, widen perspectives, change attitudes, improve social skills and develop alternative solutions to problems. Role playing is perhaps the next best thing to experiencing a genuine event. It does, however, have some advantages over real life situations in that timing can be made artificially rapid, situations rarely encountered can be acted out, and the learner can receive constructive feedback from supportive colleagues. Mistakes can also be made in a safe environment. Rogers states:

> In role play mistakes can be made without retribution. The atmosphere of calm analysis and good-humoured support from tutor and other students makes it possible to see why mistakes have been made and to learn to avoid them in the future. (1989: 132)

By means of role-play exercises learners may come to appreciate how complex decisions are made, for example whether to place a disabled child in a special or a mainstream school. Using this example, each learner might be given a different role to play: the father, the mother, the child, the siblings, various school teachers, health professionals and so on. This has the potential to broaden the learners' knowledge, give sensitive insight into the issue and bring about attitude change. Role play can also be used to help learners gain skill and sensitivity when helping people face stressful or difficult situations, for example when interacting with those who are terminally ill or newly disabled. Rogers states:

> Because role playing usually arouses powerful emotions in those who take part, it can be a potent and valuable method to any teacher whose subject involves sensitivity and tolerance. (1989: 133)

Role play can also be used to help learners gain skills in treating, assessing and interviewing patients and clients, and to gain confidence when talking to groups or coping with difficult personal situations; it is used extensively in assertiveness training. With this type of role play learners frequently work in pairs. Dickson et al. (1991) believe that role play has the following functions:

— to stimulate thought
— to consolidate learning
— to enhance interpersonal skills
— to heighten self-awareness
— to change attitudes
— to enhance understanding of complex situations
— to increase confidence
— to heighten sensitivity to the needs and feelings of others

— to facilitate integration of theory and practice
— to stimulate active involvement in the learning process
— to provide opportunities for problem solving and decision making
— to familiarize learners with situations they will have to cope with later

It should be appreciated, however, that, as Stevenson and Parsloe point out 'many people hate role-playing and far from gaining in self assurance become increasingly defensive' (1993: 56). The task of the therapist is to assess the mood of the group and to provide a supportive atmosphere.

Conducting the role play

A suitable room must be found for the role play to take place; a few 'props' may assist, for example a plinth for a bed, but nothing elaborate is needed. More important than the physical arrangements is the psychological atmosphere: many people are uncomfortable about the method and feel embarrassed at the thought of playing the roles because, as Rogers puts it, 'it seems to bear a suspicious resemblance to amateur dramatics' (1989: 136). The role play will only succeed if the learners are relaxed and feel psychologically secure. It is probably best avoided until the therapist and learners know each other reasonably well.

The therapist can allocate the roles to be played or can request volunteers; those not involved in the role play may be asked to observe. The observation can be structured, unstructured or semi-structured. With structured observation the observers may tick boxes on a chart every time a particular behaviour occurs, for example when the 'therapist' asks a 'leading' question during a clinical interview, or when the 'patient' or 'client' misunderstands. With unstructured or semi-structured observation the observers and participants may report on their general impressions of the encounter, although they may be asked to focus on specific themes. The role play may be video recorded for later viewing and discussion. An alternative strategy is for the learners to work in pairs or small groups without an audience and, when the role play is complete, to report back to the whole group.

Emotions can sometimes become intense in role play; the therapist should be prepared for this and ready to diffuse the situation if necessary, though it rarely gets out of control. A more common problem is resistance on the part of learners who feel embarrassed by the method. This can sometimes result in trivialization or displacement of the topic. If this occurs the therapist should calmly stop the role play and remind learners of its purpose and their roles within it.

A discussion can take place after the role play, led either by the therapist or the learners. The observers can report their findings and impressions, and attitudes, feelings and behaviour can be analysed. Constructive feedback can be given and the relevance of the knowledge to practice emphasized. When role play is successful it is often very difficult to bring it to a close.

It is possible for therapists to use this teaching method even if they only have an hour or two to spare. It can be tremendously successful and rewarding, although its success depends, to a large degree, on the motivation of the learners. Failure is unlikely, however, if careful thought, planning and explanation are given. It is often the case at courses and conferences that the various speakers fail to discuss their teaching methods with each other, thus the learners are presented with the same method, usually the lecture, time and again. If therapists can find the courage to attempt an unconventional teaching method their message is likely to be remembered well, not only because of the active nature of the learning, but because of the novelty value of the method.

Simulation (case studies)

The terms 'simulation' and 'case study' are used interchangeably. Jones (1987) believes that classroom simulations have two essential characteristics: first that the learners have functional roles, for example that of a doctor or therapist, and second that sufficient information is provided to enable them to function as professionals. He states: 'if, before the observer arrived, the participants had spent some time delving into the facts about the issue and were thinking professionally, then it would be a simulation' (1987: 12). Curzon refers to simulations as case studies, which he describes as being 'based upon the examination, analysis and diagnosis of a real or simulated problem so that general principles might emerge in a realistic fashion' (1990: 295).

An example of a simulation exercise might be the short-listing of candidates for a job. After explaining the task very carefully, the therapist will provide each learner with relevant documentation of fictitious but realistic candidates. The learners will first be asked to read and digest the information, and then to meet in small groups to discuss and agree upon which candidates to select, perhaps three out of ten. Each group then presents its conclusions and justifies its decisions. The precise format of the simulation is adjusted to suit specific requirements.

The method could also be used to highlight the complexities of planning rehabilitation programmes for specific patients or clients. The learners could take on the roles of various health professionals and be provided with documentation relating to a patient's or client's physical, social and psychological circumstances which could be followed by a case conference.

The method has been used most extensively on management courses, and as a means of assessing people's skills when recruiting them for various occupations. They may, for example, be asked to solve a problem within a group context with inadequate information, or cope with a difficult situation in a leadership role. Every simulation is different according to its objectives. If the learners are asked to solve a complex problem with a right or wrong answer, an element of competition is introduced, in which case it is an example of an academic game.

Simulation exercises are sometimes carried out in an attempt to gain insight into various disabilities, for example the participants may be obliged to wear blindfolds or use wheelchairs. These exercises have been severely criticized by many disabled people for being unrealistic, for trivializing and individualizing disability, and for fostering negative attitudes. They are rarely used by disability equality trainers who are, themselves, disabled. (For a full discussion and a critique of these exercises, see French, 1992.)

Conducting the simulation

Jones (1987) believes that teachers should remain detached while the simulation is in progress. Simulations provide experiential learning where mistakes are inevitable and desirable and should be allowed to occur. There is a place for the therapist to intervene if things go badly wrong, but this should be done unobtrusively and, if possible, within an appropriate role. For example, if a vital document is missing when carrying out a simulation exercise, the therapist could bring it to the person concerned in the role of an apologetic messenger (Jones 1987).

The demands on the therapist are considerable with this method. The preparation of suitable materials takes time and effort and demands the use of resources such as photocopying facilities. However, if the material is retained it can be used again, or alternatively the learners may produce their own materials as part of the exercise. It is very important that the documents are relevant and that nothing is missing or the exercise will not succeed. The layout of the furniture should also be appropriate to the task. Timing must be strictly adhered to, there is nothing worse than a simulation being interrupted in the middle unless it is designed to last for long periods.

As with role play, it is usual practice to discuss the simulation when it is complete, to draw out the main principles and to link the issues raised with past and future learning. The discussion can either be led by the therapist or by one or more of the learners.

Conclusion

It is possible for therapists to use role play and simulation even if they only have one teaching session. They are more risky than structured teaching approaches, such as the lecture, as they are less predictable, but if they work well the learners are likely to assimilate and remember a great deal, as they are so actively involved.

Chapter

11

Supervising Projects

The quality of supervision is, arguably, the single most important factor in successful undertaking of research. (Brown and Atkins, 1988: 127)

Therapists are increasingly required to help learners with their projects. Projects may be carried out by individuals, for example undergraduate research projects, or the therapist may require a pair or a group of learners to carry out a project jointly, for example during a clinical or fieldwork placement. A group project may be appropriate if the therapist is responsible for two or more learners for a considerable period of time. With any project it is usually expected that at least some of the work will be done outside clinical or college hours.

Supervising individual projects

Involvement in the supervision of a learner's project is a serious and demanding activity which should not be undertaken without considerable thought and commitment. Although it is unlikely to take up an enormous amount of time, the time allocated to it must be adequate. The therapist must be available to see learners fairly regularly although the amount of supervision they want or need will differ. Brown and Atkins (1988) believe that relying on learners to ask for help is risky because they may not know what questions to ask, and may be loath to appear inadequate or demanding.

Undertaking a piece of research alone can be very isolating, and any feelings of isolation which develop can easily lead to lack of confidence, poor motivation and low self-esteem. Regular and constructive contact with the therapist will help to prevent or alleviate these feelings. The therapist can also arrange seminars and discussion groups among several learners where their work can be presented and their ideas exchanged. (For information on seminars and discussion groups, the reader is referred to chapters 8 and 9.)

The learner/therapist relationship

The relationship between the therapist and the learner undertaking a project is a personal one which is based on partnership. It is important that the relationship is friendly, open and supportive, and that the therapist is concerned about the personal well-being of the learner as well as his or her academic achievements. All decisions should be made jointly with learners. Brown and Atkins state:

> The good supervisor is concerned for the general well-being and intellectual growth of the student, and not just with the mechanics of the project . . . a comfortable, safe atmosphere has to be created together with the expectation of regular, planned and structured work. (1988: 131)

It is important during meetings to avoid telephone conversations and other interruptions; to do so will convey respect, interest and concern. The arrangement of the furniture should be conducive to informal discussion; conducting some of the meetings over lunch or coffee can provide a relaxed and friendly atmosphere.

Carrying out a research project is intellectually taxing and stressful as new skills and techniques must be mastered, and deadlines met. Research also has a dreary and monotonous side, for example when feeding data into a computer, addressing hundreds of envelopes, or transcribing interviews from tape. Phillips and Pugh (1987) believe that part of the supervisor's role is to keep the learners' morale high and to demonstrate an understanding of both the emotional and the intellectual problems they face. Brown and Atkins (1988) cite evidence to show that the preferred supervisory style is one providing warmth and structure, whereas the least preferred style is one exhibiting coldness and lack of organization.

The dynamics of the relationship should be discussed regularly. It is essential for therapists to know what the learners expect of them and whether this tallies with their own expectations. It must be established, for example, whether both people are happy with the regularity of the meetings, and whether the learner feels the therapist is giving too much or too little help. An informal contract needs to be negotiated and revised as the project progresses to ensure that no major problems ensue. Learners will need different types of assistance from therapists according to the stage of the project reached and how much confidence and expertise has been gained. No two learners and no two projects are ever the same, which makes supervision demanding, yet interesting and rewarding.

What makes a good project supervisor?

The role of project supervisor is complex and there is much disagreement about its precise nature, not only between learners and supervisors but among supervisors themselves. There may be disagreement, for example, about the amount of help learners should be given, how often meetings should take place, and how much responsibility learners should take for their own projects. Brown and Atkins (1988) list many aspects of the supervisor's role including that of director, facilitator, adviser, teacher, critic, supporter, friend, manager, examiner and guide. Supervisors often find themselves cast in the role of counsellor: reducing learners' anxieties, and assuring them that all is well.

It is important that therapists have a good grasp of the subject matter of the learners' projects and the methods they will be using, indeed this is usually the main reason why specific people are chosen to supervise particular projects. It is not necessary, however, to have a detailed knowledge of the *precise* question the learner is investigating; the topic may, in fact, be original.

Learners should be free to use the expertise of other members of staff; part of the therapist's role is to facilitate access to them, as well as other useful resources, such as literature, lectures and conferences. Therapists may also seek permission, on the learners' behalf, for the research to take place, assist with the presentation of proposals to ethics committees, and introduce the learners to suitable patients and clients who are willing to act as research participants.

Whatever stage learners have reached with their projects, meetings must be thoughtfully planned and well structured. At the end of each meeting realistic short-term goals should be set so that learners know exactly what to do and where they are heading. The date and the purpose of the next meeting should also be decided. Any work the learner leaves with the therapist should be read well in advance and con-structive comments given.

Initially the learner will be concerned with choosing a topic and formulating aims and objectives. The role of the therapist at this stage is to provide encouragement and to help to draw out and clarify the learner's thoughts and ideas; learners should be directed to suitable references, resources and organizations. Research seminars and discussions with other learners are very helpful in achieving these aims. As the project progresses the issues discussed will become more specific, although the aims of the project as a whole should always be kept in mind. If it is a research project the learner may want advice and discussion on what research methods to use, how to carry out the research, and how to analyse the findings. The final goal of the learner is to write the project up, a task which many find daunting. The therapist should be prepared to see the drafts which the learner produces and give detailed and constructive guidance regarding their improve-ment. (For further information on writing research projects, readers are referred to French and Sim, 1993; and French, 1993.)

Help from others, for example a statistician or someone experienced in constructing questionnaires, may become necessary or desirable. It is unlikely that any one therapist will possess all the necessary expertise to help with every aspect of the learner's project, indeed at the present time therapists are likely to be working in collaboration with academic staff. It is not good practice to be in sole charge of a research project without practical research experience oneself, or a knowledge of the methods to be used. Many projects are jointly supervised, but even then outside help is frequently sought.

In order to succeed and reach a high standard of work, learners require detailed feedback, including criticism. Giving criticism is difficult and must be done constructively. Phillips and Pugh state:

> It is the supervisor's job to criticise and provide feedback but the manner in which the information is given is absolutely vital. If the criticism is harsh, or perceived as such by the student, untold damage can be done. (1987: 105)

As a general rule criticism must be very specific and focused on particular problems rather than on the learner's personality or overall ability. Clear and detailed guidance on how to overcome the problems should be given. Thus, rather than saying 'this questionnaire is awful, you need to write it again', the therapist should specify exactly what is wrong with the questionnaire: perhaps some of the questions are ambiguous, perhaps there are too many open-ended questions, or insufficient space for the respondent to write. The learner should be given one or two concrete examples of how to improve it and directed to some suitable references. It is rare for a learner's work to be wholly bad, and criticism can usually be combined with praise for aspects of the work which have been done well.

In order to avoid feelings of failure when work is not up to standard, it helps to let people know in advance just how difficult or time-consuming a task is likely to be. When the learners come to write up their projects, for example, the therapist could tell them at the outset that most people need to write several drafts before it is acceptable, and that the usual practice is for the project to pass backwards and forwards between learner and supervisor several times.

A common problem is for the project to become too big, unmanageable and expensive. The therapist should endeavour to prevent this from happening without reducing the learner's motivation. The unwieldiness of a project is usually apparent from the first meeting, although the recognition of this may only come with experience. Qualitative research, in particular, usually takes longer than inexperienced researchers imagine.

Supervising group projects

As well as supervising individual projects, therapists may ask two learners, or a group of learners, to carry out a project together. They may, for example, give the learners a month to discover what facilities exist for children with cerebral palsy in the community. Once the information has been collected they may require the learners to write their findings up and present them to other learners in a stimulating way.

The amount of help therapists give will depend on the seniority of the learners and their previous experience. They may or may not be allocated specific roles or be told exactly what to investigate. It is likely that some guidance will be necessary, not only in carrying out the study, but also with its presentation; for example the learners may seek assistance in preparing audio-visual materials, writing a handout, or preparing a lecture or discussion group. Therapists are obviously at an advantage if they are well versed in a range of teaching methods.

Group project work is demanding and can be expensive, but with adequate guidance and group cohesion it is a very stimulating way to learn, and lacks the loneliness associated with individual project work. It is a particularly good way of capitalizing on the skill and knowledge of individual group members. For example, one person may have a flair for interviewing, another for photography, a third for statistics and someone else for public speaking. Rogers (1989) gives many examples of excellent group projects produced by learners in local-authority adult education classes.

As well as learning and developing their own skills, people learn a great deal from other group members. If all goes well something really worth while can result: perhaps a research report, a health education booklet, a piece of equipment, or a teaching aid. Poor motivation is not usually a difficulty, as Rogers states: 'the whole tormented "problem" of wringing "written work" from students fades away in the context of a project' (1989: 162). Although group project work may take time to set up, and be more demanding than most teaching methods, the learners are likely to derive a great deal of satisfaction from it, and will almost certainly learn and retain more than they would by more conventional means.

A good project supervisor is flexible, adaptable and full of ideas, someone who can motivate learners and who does not panic when things go wrong. Supervising projects is very rewarding work; much of the contact is on a one-to-one basis, which leads to a real sense of partnership as well as excitement and satisfaction when a good piece of work is produced.

Conclusion

Expertise in supervising projects is becoming more important for therapists. Students and junior therapists often depend on the help and goodwill of clinicians when carrying out projects as part of their course work or clinical role. Help and discussion with clinicians, experienced in the particular area concerned, is not only valuable, but often essential. As more therapists undertake degree programmes, and as research in the clinical setting becomes more common, the role of therapists in the supervision of projects will inevitably increase and their skill in this area will become even more important.

Chapter

12

Teaching Practical Skills

Practical skills are widely used in therapy. There are the fine gradations of movement used in passive manual mobilization techniques applied to peripheral or spinal joints, the manipulation of soft tissues used in massage, and the specialized neuromuscular facilitation techniques used, for example, in the re-education of facial musculature. Practical skills are also needed to lift patients or clients safely and to assist them with functional activities such as feeding, dressing, transferring from bed to chair, and walking. The use of electromedical apparatus, the making and application of splints, the setting up of a range of exercise equipment, and the performance of assessment procedures, such as laryngoscopy and muscle testing, also require dextrous handling.

Three major processes can be identified in motor, i.e. practical, skill acquisition: knowing what to do, knowing how to do it, and adapting to the environment in which the skill is performed (Colley, 1989). Knowing what to do is concerned with understanding the task or goal, it relies heavily on verbal instruction. Knowing how to execute the skill is dependent on performing it and feeling what it is like. With practice and feedback to correct any errors that are made, the efficient sequencing of movement is developed. Finally, when a level of competency has been reached, further practice may result in a fluency of movement which is one of the hallmarks of skilled performance.

There is an extensive literature, in the fields of psychology and sports training, which elaborate these processes (Adams, 1987; Colley and Beech, 1989). There is also much debate about the precise learning mechanisms involved. It is, however, beyond the scope of this chapter to examine these arguments in depth; instead a practical stance will be taken which will provide therapists with strategies to adopt when teaching practical skills. (For an overview of learning theories, the reader is referred to chapter 1.)

Learning by observation and instruction

One of the ways in which a therapist might begin to teach a practical skill is to demonstrate it to the learners while, at the same time, carefully explaining it. For observation and instruction to succeed, it is essential that learners are motivated and attentive. It is usually best to demonstrate the entire sequence first; it is vital that the demonstration is fluent and of a high standard. If the therapist has not practised the skill recently, or if the equipment is unfamiliar, then time must be spent rehearsing the skill beforehand. Thought is also needed on how best to teach the activity. It is frequently the case that the skilled practice of therapists becomes almost automatic, making it difficult for them to describe or explain precisely what they are doing.

Following the demonstration of the whole skill, it should be broken down into its component parts, and each part taught separately (Curzon, 1990). Learners should be encouraged to watch the demonstration from different physical angles; the therapist should also change position, moving to the other side of the model, for example. Changing position is important because it usually involves changing hand contact, stance and posture. It is unlikely that the learners will perceive or remember every aspect of the demonstration initially, so the therapist should repeat it several times, highlighting areas of confusion which may occur. Giving verbal instruction and demonstrating the skill at the same time is preferable to either mode of instruction in isolation, as the more sensory channels that are used the better the learning. This having been said, care must be taken not to overload the learner with too much information. Verbal instruction should always complement the demonstration.

Practice and feedback

While observation and instruction are useful as starting points for learning, they should rapidly give way to practice. It is only through active participation that learners will understand, for example, where to place their hands, how much pressure to apply, and how to operate the apparatus. Proprioceptive feedback from their own muscles will also enhance the learning of the skill, particularly with movements which require some degree of postural adjustment (Colley, 1989). The learners should be encouraged to practise assiduously; therapists often underestimate the length of time it takes to master practical skills.

Feedback from the therapist, in the form of correction, is an essential aspect of practical skills teaching and learning. In order to give useful feedback the therapist needs to analyse the skill in detail. If it is difficult to acquire and feedback is not forthcoming, learners tend to lose interest. The therapist should move around the room and assist the learners individually. If the group is larger than twenty then the assistance of a second therapist is useful. Periodically the whole group should be observed to get an idea of how interested and motivated the learners seem, and how well they are learning the skill. It may be that some general errors are emerging, or the therapist may recognize that a specific aspect of the demonstration should have been emphasized. If this is the case the whole group can be asked to watch the therapist demonstrate the skill again. It is useful to perform it on a different model each time so that as many learners as possible have an opportunity to feel the therapist's performance. Feedback from the learners concerning, for example, the difficulties they are encountering, is also important.

It is vital to point out or demonstrate the errors in a learner's performance. Studies have shown that the more detail learners are given about the errors they make the more readily they are able to correct them (Adams, 1987; Annett, 1989). Being told, for example, to use body weight more, will be less useful to learners than instructing them to transfer their body weight from the back leg to the front leg. Similarly, being told that a movement is too fast, is less useful than observing the correct speed or being asked to slow the speed by half.

There are a number of ways in which the learner's performance can be corrected. The therapist may give verbal instruction or demonstrate the skill on the model with the learner watching. An alternative strategy is for the therapist's hands to be placed on top of the learner's to facilitate the correct movement, pressure, rhythm or speed. The therapist may also use the learner as a model so that the correct procedure can be felt directly. Once the separate parts of a complex skill are mastered, the learners should practise combining the various components using correct timing. While correction is essential for learning, it is equally important to give praise where it is due, praise is a powerful motivator for any learner grappling with new activities and practical procedures.

When learners are practising in pairs, the model should be encouraged to give feedback, particularly in terms of how the skill felt, and whether it felt similar or dissimilar to the way the therapist performed it. This not only helps the learner, but increases the interest of the model too. Patients may also be asked their opinions regarding the comfort, or otherwise, of the learner's performance. Learners need to practise their skills on a range of body types and changing partners should be a strategy adopted in any practical skills teaching session.

If learners are working in small groups, using apparatus for example, those observing can be asked to give feedback. This not only helps to maintain their attention, but develops their powers of observation. They could even be asked to rate the performance they observe against some agreed set of criteria thus introducing an element of peer assessment. This is particularly useful in helping learners to recognize good standards of practice.

The learners should be encouraged to practise in between the teaching sessions. Provided they are aware of how the skill should be performed, this can result in an improvement despite a lack of feedback from the therapist. For improvement to occur, however, the learner's internal feedback must be adequate (Adams, 1987). Video recordings of the skill can, if necessary, be made available and will go some way to providing the necessary guidance.

If learners are unable to practise physically, then mental practice can be useful. Learners should be asked to rehearse the skill mentally, attempting to produce a vivid visual image as well as the 'feel' of the skill. Studies have shown that this is a useful strategy to adopt and, when combined with periods of physical practice, can result in a more rapid acquisition of motor skills (Warner and McNeill, 1988; Maring, 1990). Watts (1990) suggests that this strategy can also be used during the teaching of the skill when learners can be asked to practise mentally while watching the therapist's demonstration.

Individual differences

When teaching practical skills it is not unusual to find that learners vary in the time it takes to achieve an acceptable standard. For some, learning the new skill may appear to come naturally, while for others there may be confusion and delay. One factor behind these differences could be the learner's existing experience and the extent to which it either facilitates or inhibits the new learning. The influence of one activity (the previous experience) on the performance of another activity is known as transfer of training (Adams, 1987). When there is a degree of similarity between the new skill and the skills already learned, facilitation may occur, resulting in the new skill being acquired more readily. Learners who have acquired the skill of making resting splints with plaster of Paris, for example, may readily transfer this skill to using a different type of material. They already know how to handle the limb, what position they want the limb held in, and how to protect any vulnerable areas. They can, therefore, concentrate on working with the different properties of the new splinting material. Being aware of the implications of transfer of training can help the therapist to give sympathetic guidance to the learners.

On the other hand, a new skill which is very similar to a previously learned skill may result in confusion and inhibition of the learning. Various ways in which a physiotherapist handles limbs when performing exercise techniques, for example, may be confusing to learners until they have sorted out the subtle differences among them. It is a useful strategy to ask learners to what extent the new learning is similar to previously learned activity. It may then be possible to point out in advance those aspects that can be usefully transferred, or to highlight possible difficulties which, by being made explicit, can be avoided.

Another influence on the learning of practical skills may concern learners' physical characteristics, such as height, arm length and whether they are left or right handed. In some of the exercise techniques and handling procedures used by therapists, for example the ways in which patients are supported, alternative methods may need to be identified. The learners themselves may be able to recognize and apply these alternatives, while maintaining the basic principles of the activity.

Other influences on individual performance concern the learners' natural ability to learn practical skills, and their degree of interest and motivation. (For further information on individual differences in learning, the reader is referred to chapter 1.)

Structure of practical classes

The acquisition of practical skills is a relatively slow process which needs considerable practice. Practice is tolerated better in short, rather than long, periods; it is the responsibility of the therapist to identify a suitable 'chunk' of skill which can be acquired within the time available. Curzon (1990) suggests that 60 per cent of class time should be used for guided practice, 25 per cent for demonstration, and 15 per cent for verbal explanation. Regardless of how the class is arranged there will always be variability among the learners concerning the pace of their learning. The therapist should be sufficiently flexible to cope with this.

Learners who find it easy to perform the skill may practise with a different partner, or be enlisted as assistants (Watts, 1990). Another strategy is for them to participate in discovery learning where, for example, they may determine how the skill could be performed with different muscles, joints, or starting positions. It may be appropriate to set up a number of 'practice stations', each with written instructions, through which learners rotate. This is particularly useful for revision at the end of a series of skills classes.

Conclusion

The acquisition of practical skills forms an important part of a practitioner's work and requires learners to spend sufficient time practising in order to develop an acceptable standard. It is the responsibility of the therapist to provide an encouraging and supportive environment so that learners feel comfortable and safe to make mistakes, particularly in the early stages of learning. Learners may spend a great deal of time practising on each other and although this results in a certain standard being achieved it is only the beginning. Working with patients and clients with various illnesses and impairments offers more challenges, and learners will need to adjust their skills to the different conditions presented.

13

Clinical Teaching

Clinical teaching can be the greatest, yet the most rewarding, challenge for therapists. It is in the hospital or community setting that learners are enabled to develop the necessary clinical skills and come to recognize the standards and behaviours of their chosen profession (Wolf, 1980). This is particularly so if learners are undertaking their pre-qualifying course, but other learners may require just as much assistance. These may include therapists returning to the clinical field after a period of absence, or those from overseas who need help to adjust to a different health care system. In such situations it is likely that the teacher, that is the senior therapist, will have responsibility for one or two learners, as well as responsibility for the needs of the service. It will be necessary to strike a balance between these two commitments.

When working with such small numbers of learners in the clinical setting, interpersonal skills are of paramount importance (Emery, 1984; Jarski et al., 1989). A friendly welcome goes a long way to putting the learner at ease, and effort on the part of the therapist to develop an atmosphere of mutual trust and collaboration will facilitate the learning process. Not only may learners feel anxious about how they will relate to their supervisors, but in the case of pre-qualified learners it is in the clinical situation that they encounter patients and clients for the first time. In this situation they are often fearful of causing pain or 'doing the wrong thing'. More experienced learners may also feel some degree of unease due to the unfamiliarity of the new clinical area.

Preparation

Although a great deal of teaching and learning in the clinical situation is opportunistic, being dependent on patient or client availability, a certain amount of planning can help to maximize the learning experience. Before the learners arrive it will help if the therapist has already organized some time to spend with them, perhaps by asking colleagues to rearrange their work loads. An information pack which could include a map of the hospital or community unit, a list of the names of doctors or social service staff with whom the learners will come into contact, and details of health and safety policies, will be a useful resource (Stengelhofen, 1993). A timetable setting out the proposed learning activities will be an additional help, at least for the early part of the learning experience. Learners are often overwhelmed by the sheer quantity of information presented on their first day and may find it difficult to remember everything.

Not only should the therapist prepare for the forthcoming clinical placement, but the learners have a responsibility to do the same. On a pre-qualifying course the learners should revise the necessary aspects of theory covered in college. Learners returning to their profession after a break in service may have received some reading material in advance.

The therapist will need to think about specific learning objectives that could be offered, and the learners should consider what knowledge and skills they need to acquire. In the early days of the clinical placement some time should be set aside to discuss any previous relevant experience the learners have had, as well as their expectations of the clinical placement. Details of how these objectives and expectations might be achieved could form part of a learning contract. (For further information on setting objectives and negotiating a learning contract, the reader is referred to chapter 4.)

Learning from practice

Learning from clinical experience is a process which links work, education and personal development. Learning how to learn is an important goal, particularly at the present time when the knowledge base of many professions grows and changes rapidly. Kolb (1984) describes a learning cycle which illustrates how such learning may be achieved.

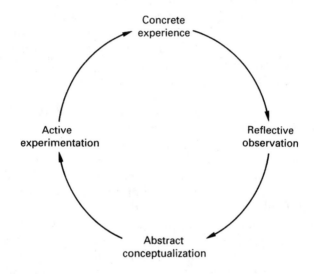

Figure 13.1 *Kolb's learning cycle (1984)*

The process of 'doing' (concrete experience) is followed by noting what 'happened' and what was 'felt' (reflective observation). Reflective observation gives meaning to what has occurred; it is insufficient merely to have the experience since, if it is not reflected upon, it is likely to be forgotten (Gibbs, 1988). Linking the experience with prior knowledge or identifying new theory to make sense of the experience (abstract conceptualization) is followed by 'testing out' the new understanding in different situations (active experimentation) which, in turn, leads back to concrete experience.

Imagine some learners in a rehabilitation unit for older people where they are expected to treat a number of clients with walking problems. The learners may know about the pathological conditions of the clients, as well as the importance of psychological and social factors in their treatment, from theory learned in college. They may have in mind a certain repertoire of skills that might be offered. It is only during exposure to practice, however, that they come to recognize the uniqueness of each individual and how they themselves relate to each, and the need to develop a variety of treatment and communication strategies. What may work effectively for one client may not work effectively for another, or the same pathological condition may manifest itself in diverse ways or have very different outcomes.

The learners must come to recognize the multidimensional nature of patients' and clients' problems and develop different strategies to assist with each. This not only illustrates how learning emerges from practice, but it demonstrates that some knowledge can only be gained through practice, what Schön (1983) calls 'knowing-in-action'. Reflection is the key here whereby learners become aware of what is taking place through dialogue with the experience (Bond and Walker 1990). Keeping a diary or learning log can be useful in enabling learners to stand back from the clinical experience and identify what has been learned. Learners may also help each other by spending time together reflecting on and sharing their experiences. The therapist should encourage these activities and be instrumental in helping learners progress around the learning cycle.

The supervisory role

The style of teaching adopted by the therapist will be critical to the process of learning. It is likely that the therapist will need to adjust to different learners, and to adapt to them as their needs change. Most learners will require a great deal of direction initially and will want to watch the therapist in action to observe, for example, skilled applications of manual techniques or the use of complex equipment. The learners will also want to see how the therapist interacts on a professional level with patients, clients and colleagues. The therapist provides a role model, particularly for the pre-qualified learner. This in itself can be stressful, especially if the therapist is new to the teaching role (Munroe, 1988). Although it is necessary for the therapist to set a good example, the learner must appreciate that the therapist is not infallible; both should acknowledge that there are different ways of doing things.

A danger in this early period of learning is that learners are placed in a passive role; it is important that they participate as soon as possible. Perhaps they could work alongside the therapist carrying out some aspects of the treatment. Provided the right approach is adopted the relationship between the learner and the patient or client should not be undermined. These interpersonal skills are, however, often ones which both the learner and the therapist need to develop; the therapist learning how to intervene with sensitivity, and the learner learning to accept the necessary interventions of the therapist.

Another way in which learners can be encouraged to participate in the early stages of their clinical education is during discussion with the therapist, when the learners' opinions can be sought concerning the clinical problems encountered. Learners could be asked to justify both their choice of treatment and any advice they might give, and be encouraged to offer alternative strategies. This not only develops critical thinking in the learners, but the therapist becomes aware of how much knowledge and understanding they have, which is useful for subsequent planning. Handal and Lauvås (1987) make the point that the teacher should take the skills and knowledge of learners as the starting point of the learning experience.

Once learners feel sufficiently confident to practise alone, and the therapist is satisfied with their level of ability, this should be allowed, with the therapist available for advice if any difficulties arise. It is an important step for learners to work independently. The therapist is still responsible for them, but the learners also have a duty not to undertake any work for which training has not been received. A useful stratagem is for therapists to ask learners to explain their intentions and then to allow them to practise. It is helpful, bearing in mind the availability of patients and clients, for the therapist to structure learners' experiences so that relatively simple clinical problems are seen and practised before more complex ones.

The final step in the supervisory sequence is for therapists to join the learners again, but this time as observers, while the learners are practitioners. In this way therapists can give useful feedback to learners about their developing skills. Feedback should be given as soon as possible after the observation. It is preferable for therapists to accept the learners' practice, if it is of an acceptable standard, even though it might not be exactly the same as their own. Learners tend to find it unhelpful when therapists take over. As Handal and Lauvås say 'the task of the supervisor is not to do the job for the student but to help the student master the job he is practising' (1987: 3). It is also beneficial to encourage learners to evaluate their own practice.

A criticism often voiced by learners is that therapists do not observe them sufficiently or give them enough feedback on their practice. In some situations being observed could alter the delicate interaction between learner and client, for example, while working with those with learning difficulties. In situations such as these a video recording could be used which the learner and therapist might discuss in private. It may also be possible to observe the learner from a distance, or to listen from an adjacent cubicle.

It is clear that the success of the supervisory role is dependent upon the interaction which develops between therapist and learner. The therapist is usually required to adopt a directive style of supervision initially, but as the learner gains confidence it is more useful for the therapist to become a facilitator, a resource to whom the learner can turn for guidance (Gardiner, 1989). As a facilitator the focus is on the learner's abilities and the learner is given support and time to consolidate what has been learned. It is important that both therapist and learner are motivated and feel positive towards each other. If the relationship between them is seriously strained then learning will be inhibited. If such a situation arises it is better for the learner to work with another therapist.

Other learning activities

Although the major part of clinical teaching is concerned with the contact learners have with their patients and clients, there are many other activities which can enhance learning and provide greater insight into the overall provision of care. Ward conferences and multidisciplinary team meetings are invaluable ways for learners to appreciate an holistic approach. They should be encouraged to contribute to these gatherings. Time spent observing diagnostic and surgical procedures can improve knowledge of underlying theory, and attendance at clinics can give learners an appreciation of a wide variety of clinical problems and the treatments available.

Therapists may choose to organize tutorials and seminars focusing on the learners' current practice. This will help learners link theory with practice and focus their thinking on the process of clinical decision making, rather than diseases or operative procedures *per se*. Similarly the requirement to document all aspects of the care episode will help learners to develop analytical skills and clinical reasoning abilities. (For further information on tutorials and seminars, the reader is referred to chapter 8.)

Conclusion

Teaching clinical skills is demanding and requires therapists to manage their time carefully in order to accommodate this important educational responsibility into their clinical role. Preparation beforehand, negotiation of the learning goals with learners, and the development of a climate of support and mutual trust, will help adult learners to become responsible and independent practitioners. Such an experience is likely to be highly rewarding for therapists and learners alike.

Part Four

Assessment and Evaluation

14

Assessing Learners

Of all the teaching skills which the therapist needs to develop, the skills of assessment possibly arouse the greatest apprehension. The desire to give a fair assessment is often voiced, and implicit in this desire is the fear of judging a learner too harshly. Giving a learner a fail grade can be as upsetting for the therapist as it is for the learner who receives it.

There are many factors to consider before the assessment process is chosen. It is helpful to think about the following questions:

(1) What is the purpose of the assessment?
(2) What should be assessed?
(3) How should the assessment be conducted?
(4) Who should be involved in the assessment process?

Assessment should be considered when planning the entire teaching programme, rather than being tagged on at the end as an afterthought.

The purpose of assessment

When a group of therapists were asked during an assessment workshop in 1990 to consider why assessment needed to be carried out, they felt that well-planned assessment should discover the learner's strengths and weaknesses, help the learner to develop, maintain professional standards, encourage the learner, identify gaps in knowledge and give feedback. These responses fall into two broad categories. First there is the need to be diagnostic, to identify what the learner can do well and what needs to be improved, and second there is the need to judge, to act as 'gatekeeper' so that standards do not fall. The diagnostic purpose of assessment is known as formative assessment implying that further help will be given to the learner. It is intended to help the learner to grow and it places the therapist in the role of facilitator. The judgement aspect of assessment is known as summative assessment and is used to measure what has been learned (Rowntree, 1979). The teaching in this case is considered to be complete and the therapist is put into the role of judge.

It is likely that all therapists who are involved in a teaching capacity will be concerned with formative assessment. When practical skills are taught and clinical practice is supervised the feedback given by the therapist is dependent on the therapist having assessed the learner. This is often an informal and continuing process. At the end of the period of teaching, if the therapist is asked to grade the learner, then the assessment will be summative. However, the boundaries may not always be quite so distinct. A summative assessment at the end of a period of supervised practice usually carries with it some recommendations that the learner needs to address in subsequent practice placements, and as such may also be seen as formative assessment.

Another aspect to consider regarding these two purposes of assessment is the effect on the therapist of being both facilitator and judge. The therapist and the learner will have got to know each other well through working together and this may reduce the anxiety often felt when judging and being judged. This, in turn, may lead to a fairer assessment. However, it could be argued that the therapist may be biased in favour of the learner, or if there has been a personality clash, biased against the learner. Another effect of a poor relationship between the therapist and the learner is the likelihood that the learner will be reticent with the therapist, not wanting to reveal inadequacies and thus not gaining the maximum benefit from the learning experience (Cox and Ewan, 1988). Either way, the assessment could be influenced adversely. It is therefore important to consider how these influences may be minimized when determining what should be assessed and how the assessment should be carried out.

What should be assessed and how should assessment be conducted?

The desired outcomes of the learning programme should be carefully considered when determining how the learning should be assessed. For example, if the learner is required to develop expertise in the application of a practical skill, then it would seem sensible to require the learner to demonstrate the skill rather than write down how it might be done. If, on the other hand, it is necessary to ascertain whether or not the learner has acquired some knowledge about the use of a piece of equipment, or some understanding about the problems likely to be encountered by a patient or client, an oral presentation or a written answer would be more appropriate. Similarly, establishing if the learner has developed the necessary skills of documentation will require the therapist to scrutinize examples of record keeping.

It is well recognized that learners will be influenced by the perceptions they have of the assessment method (Gibbs and Habeshaw, 1990). The therapist should, therefore, choose methods which orientate the learner towards the desired outcomes. Attention to these points will increase the validity of the assessment process ensuring as far as possible that it is testing what it is meant to test. If the assessment method is not valid, there is a danger of making false judgements about the learner's performance which can be damaging (Newble and Cannon, 1983). Therapists may be involved with all of these methods, i.e. observation of a skill, listening to an oral presentation, reading a piece of written work. The next step is to consider how each may be judged.

Observation of a skill

This could refer to the observation of treatment to a patient or client during clinical or fieldwork experience, or the demonstration of a practical skill on a colleague while undertaking a skills course. A fundamental requirement is that the therapist will have observed enough of the learner's practice to make a judgement. It is necessary for the therapist to define the areas that need to be assessed, and then to consider what is acceptable and what is not. An example might be the use of ultrasound in physiotherapy practice. This could require the learner to think about and demonstrate assembly of apparatus, preparation of patient, preparation and testing of apparatus, instructions and warnings, treatment, termination of treatment and recording. Some of these areas can be further subdivided, for example treatment can be broken down into application, timing, observation of the patient and safety. The final checklist should be a detailed reflection of the desired practice.

The next step is to make a judgement about each area of the practice shown. For example, the treatment application needs to be accurate and comfortable while the termination of treatment should include examination of the area treated and appropriate advice to the patient. It may also be desirable to make a judgement about the overall performance in terms of efficiency and consideration given to total patient care. Additional guidance may be given by specifying clearly those elements of the treatment which fall short of expectations.

The therapist may either grade the performance on a pass/fail basis according to the presence or otherwise of the specified evidence, or allocate a mark which can be used to determine a pass or fail grade. Further sophistication may be achieved by employing a number of grades with a written explanation of each. The latter method is known as criterion referencing (Rowntree, 1979). It can minimize the personal bias which may arise in the assessment process, thus increasing both reliability and validity. The identification of criteria is far from easy, however, and it is useful to undertake the task with two or three colleagues or even with the learners.

Another method of assessment is to watch the learners perform in turn and then make a judgement by comparing them with the norm established by the group. This is known as norm referencing (Rowntree, 1979). The danger here is that the class level can fluctuate, being higher with a group of 'strong' learners and lower with a 'weak' group. Consider a piece of fieldwork experience: if a learner is perceived to be better than a previous learner who was weak, then the second learner may receive a pass grade even though the performance may have demonstrated a number of omissions. Conversely, if the first learner was strong, a subsequent learner may appear weak by comparison and thus be given a fail grade even though the performance may have been satisfactory. It is quite likely in practice that an element of norm referencing will creep in as may the desire to give credit for effort. It is possible to accommodate these influences in formative assessment, but summative assessment should be criterion referenced where it can be demonstrated that a predetermined standard has or has not been achieved.

Assessment of an oral presentation

This may be part of a clinical examination where the learner presents a case study. The learner may have been observed undertaking an assessment of a patient or client, carrying out a treatment programme or giving advice to carers. The therapist will want to discover how much the learner understands about each situation. Similarly, on a skills course, the learner may be observed carrying out a particular procedure and the therapist may want an explanation of how it may be used in practice. As with the observation of a performance, the therapist will need to have thought through carefully the evidence which will be used to determine a particular standard. The therapist may require the learner to describe concisely and comprehensively the patient's or client's functional problems, to be able to analyse them and to explain an appropriate treatment programme. Advice to carers will need to be geared to their level of understanding and the use of jargon avoided. Since the ensuing discussion is dependent as much on the skills of the therapist in eliciting the information as on the learner's ability to impart it, this method may be regarded as unreliable. Yet it may be particularly valuable to learners. Being able to talk about and justify one's actions is very much part of a therapist's work, whether the discussion is with colleagues, other professionals, patients, clients or carers. It is important to focus on what the learners know rather than what they do not know. Bligh et al. make this point when they say 'if you find a large gap in his knowledge, there is no need to find out its total extent. Change the subject' (1981: 48).

The use of open questions such as 'what ideas do you have?' and 'what do you think?' will encourage the learner to engage in discussion. The therapist's skills in assessing a learner's performance through observation or by listening and questioning will improve with practice. Reliability and validity may be further enhanced by the use of two assessors. Even if those two assessors have an agreed checklist with matching criteria, it is likely that they will perceive the performances in slightly different ways and they can then combine their interpretations to produce a fairer assessment. Another point to consider is the effect the therapist has on the learner. It is the responsibility of the therapist to try to put the learner at ease.

Written work

Although written tests are the most conventional form of assessment, it is likely that the therapist will be least involved with this method. However, some contact may occur in postgraduate and undergraduate courses. There are many different kinds of written question: these include multiple choice questions, short answer questions, essay questions and dissertations. Once again, the most reliable and valid tools to assessment are specific criteria or guidelines on which to base one's judgements. The more factual the question, the more specific the criteria can be, while the guidelines used for assessing essays and dissertations should allow room for imaginative responses and the inclusion of relevant material not necessarily thought of by the therapist. (The reader is referred to Bligh et al., 1981 for further detailed information on this topic.)

A final point worth considering with any assessment method is how practical it is in terms of time and resources.

This is particularly important in the light of the many demands made on the therapist's time.

Who should be involved in the assessment process?

Traditionally it has been the teacher who has assessed the learner, but this approach can be criticized for its onesidedness (Heron, 1988). However, it is still widely used, particularly when marking written work, though the onesidedness may be mitigated to some extent by double marking or systems which ensure anonymity. Therapists could be involved in such activity, but it is more likely that they will be concerned with the assessment of practical skills or clinical/ fieldwork experience. In such situations, having two assessors could help to reduce personal bias, but increasingly today adult learners are being encouraged to take responsibility for their own learning. The logical conclusion of this process is the involvement of the learners in the assessment process.

Self-assessment

This involves learners in the identification of goals and criteria by which they may be assessed, as well as the activity of judging the extent to which the goals have been met. Such a process will motivate and encourage learners to think about what they are doing, since the knowledge that is required to make a judgement will pervade the whole of the learning experience (Cowan, 1991); it demands that learners scrutinize their own performance and think critically about it, thus sowing the seeds for lifelong learning. This learning is particularly appealing in today's climate, with its emphasis on quality assurance. In the clinical situation, learners can be encouraged to look at their own practice and make an evaluation of it. It places the therapist in the role of facilitator, giving assistance to the learners in identifying and developing the learning goals and criteria. However, it may not be an activity to which learners readily aspire and it may take time to help them move in this direction.

Peer assessment

If the therapist is involved in assessing a group of learners, it may be useful to use peer assessment. This may develop the learners as critical thinkers and also develop their ability to work in a group (Brown and Dove 1991). They may also learn to work more effectively as part of a team. Like self-assessment, the learners are responsible for identifying goals and criteria, and initially at least, help from the therapist will be required. The judgement of the learning is then carried out, ideally in small groups of six to eight (Heron, 1988). Peer assessment is usually combined with self-assessment so that the learner being assessed has some say in the grade negotiated. If, for example, the therapist is asked to teach on a refresher course involving some form of practical skill teaching, at the end of the course peer and self-assessment could be used. Working in small groups, each learner in turn may demonstrate some of the skills that have been learned. After each demonstration, each member of the group, including the learner being assessed, might fill in a mark sheet according to an agreed set of criteria. This would then be followed by discussion during which the peer assessors, together with the learner being assessed negotiate a grade. The therapist acts as a facilitator, helping with the formulation of criteria in the first instance, and encouraging the learners to be constructive in their criticism during the negotiation stage. If learners are not familiar with this process, it is time consuming to introduce them to criteria setting and negotiation of grades, but the results are worthwhile and learners often feel they have learnt more through using this approach. It is helpful if the learners can choose their own groups, so that they feel more comfortable when giving and receiving constructive criticism.

Collaborative assessment

This is an intermediate stage between the unilateral assessment by the therapist and self-assessment by the learner. Once again, it is necessary to identify and agree a set of criteria by which the therapist and the learner can assess the learner's performance; the resultant grade is then negotiated.

This is likely to be the first step in moving away from the traditional assessment by the therapist. For pre-qualified learners, it could be a useful way of assessing clinical/ fieldwork practice, in that it encourages learner participation, yet the therapist, knowing the standards of practice, still has some degree of control. (For a more detailed account of assessment, the reader is referred to Rowntree, 1979 and Gibbs et al., 1988).

Coping with failure

Failure raises feelings of anxiety for both the learners and the therapist (Ilott, 1990) and it is important to discuss thoroughly the reasons for the failure and make explicit the evidence upon which failure is based. In the stress of the situation, the learner may not be able to accept what is being said and the interpersonal skills of the therapist are likely to be of paramount importance. Ideally, failure should never come as a total surprise. If a period of practice is being assessed, regular feedback should alert the learner to impending difficulties which may or may not be resolved by the end of the learning session. If practical skills or a case study presentation are being examined then learners who are sufficiently responsible for their own learning should be familiar with the standards expected of them and should be able to recognize a performance as below standard.

Learning may have been compromised for a number of reasons. Perhaps there was some confusion about the goals to be achieved or learners doubted their ability to achieve them. Maybe the learner had a knowledge gap or an emotional upset may have interfered with the learning. Lack of opportunity or time, or a non-supportive environment, could also impede the learning process. Whatever the reason, it is important to identify it and plan how to move forward. It is important to recognize that something positive can come out of failure as long as the failure is confronted and examined in a sensitive way. Often a combination of factors may be identified. If necessary, a third person could act as a mediator, perhaps offering a more objective view and giving support both to the therapist and the learner.

Conclusion

This chapter has looked at a number of dimensions of the assessment process. Ideally, a variety of methods should be used since each has its strengths and weaknesses. The purpose of assessment should always be carefully considered and the most appropriate method chosen with due regard to validity, reliability and practicality.

15

Evaluating the Teaching and Learning Process

Evaluation is an important aspect of the teaching and learning process. It is concerned with collecting evidence on, and making judgements about, the teaching and learning, for the purpose of improvement (Skilbeck, 1984). It concerns the extent to which the teaching and learning experience is seen to be of value (Gibby, 1978). Rowntree suggests that the role of evaluation is 'to understand our course and how learners interact with it – with a view to sustaining it, developing it and where possible, improving it' (1990: 356). Although this quotation refers to the use of open learning materials, it is equally applicable to face-to-face teaching. Evaluation is thus an essential activity if the quality of any teaching and learning programme is to be maintained or improved.

Evaluation, like assessment, should not only be addressed once the teaching has taken place, but should be considered at the planning phase and be an integral part of the teaching and learning experience. Evaluation is often confused with assessment since both are concerned with collecting evidence about what has been taught and learned; indeed the results of assessment may be used for evaluation purposes. Clinical grades, for example, could indicate something about clinical teaching, bearing in mind that other factors, such as learner motivation and availability of learning opportunities, will also be operating.

The distinguishing factor between evaluation and assessment is the use to which the evidence is put (Elton, 1984). Assessment is carried out in order to make a judgement about the standard the learner has attained, whereas evaluation is used to judge the effectiveness and satisfaction felt by the participants concerning the teaching and learning experience. It may also be used to convince others that the teaching is worthwhile, and may help teachers to see that the time allocated to planning and preparation was well spent (Rowntree, 1990). (For further information on assessment, the reader is referred to chapter 14.)

Teaching and learning are perceived in different ways. Just as learners have preferred ways of learning, therapists develop preferred ways of teaching and the two may not necessarily match. It is important to remember that one cannot please everyone all the time (Brown and Atkins, 1988). Ideally the therapist should use a range of teaching methods and adapt them according to the nature and purpose of the teaching programme; nevertheless the consequences might still be unacceptable to some learners. Evaluation is thus necessary for identifying which methods worked well and which might be improved. (For further information on individual differences in learning, the reader is referred to chapter 1.)

What should be evaluated?

A teaching encounter, whether it be a single session, a series of sessions, a short course, a conference, or a period of clinical or fieldwork practice, can be viewed as having a number of elements (Brown and Atkins, 1984; Elton, 1984). Examples of these are planning, content, teaching methods, assessment methods and learning outcomes.

Evaluative questions could be asked about the clarity and appropriateness of the aims and objectives, or the depth or difficulty of the subject matter. It is useful to find out which teaching methods were successful and which were not, and whether or not the quality of the audio-visual aids was satisfactory. Assessment methods may arouse strong feelings, and it is helpful to know whether or not the methods used are perceived by learners to be fair. Examining the actual grades achieved by the learners may also be useful when judging the extent to which the aims and objectives have been met. This, in turn, can imply something about the effectiveness of the course.

Questions can be asked about the style of teaching. The extent, for example, to which it produced a tightly-structured learning environment, or an open and collaborative one, where learners could negotiate some of the learning goals. Information should also be sought about the physical learning environment. Was the room large enough? Was there adequate seating, lighting and warmth? It may also be appropriate to ask questions about the speaker system if the lecture theatre was large and microphones were used. Therapists themselves might also want to comment on these physical aspects.

Other important issues to consider might be the support services available, such as library facilities, catering facilities and social amenities. Lack of adequate provision in any of these can lead to a general feeling of dissatisfaction. Learners who are expected to undertake private study require adequate resource material which might be available in a library or as a small collection of books and journal articles kept in a therapy department. It is also very important that learners experience a general sense of belonging, this is often engendered through informal contact with peers, over a cup of coffee in the cafeteria, or just having someone to sit with and exchange ideas.

How should evaluation be undertaken?

Informal evaluation is likely to be a continuous process which comes naturally to those therapists who are committed to education, and who strive to make their contact with learners as meaningful and successful as possible. If therapists work perceptively they are likely to receive information spontaneously from learners. Therapists may engage the learners in conversation at intervals during, or at the end of, a teaching session, asking them how they feel about particular aspects of the work. The learners may affirm that they enjoyed the session, that they found it interesting, or that it gave them confidence to practise a particular skill. If the atmosphere is supportive learners may point out difficulties or suggest what needs to be done in the next session.

A sensitive therapist will become aware of areas of difficulty by noticing whether or not the learners appear bored, and whether anyone is silent or avoiding eye contact. Being aware of non-verbal behaviour is important; indeed the therapist may modify a teaching session as it proceeds in response to the perceived reactions of the learners. Higgs (1984) suggests that as well as being sensitive to the learners, a teacher should be flexible, and willing and able to cope with any changes required. In the clinical setting problems could arise because of a mismatch of expectations between therapist and learner, or the learner may be less interested, or feel apprehensive about, the particular area of work. Being sufficiently confident to address such problems face to face, particularly with adult learners, not only assists therapists to improve such situations, but will in the long term raise their self-esteem, even though there may initially have been some painful moments. Being able to value the learner as a person is important.

There may be limited time to concentrate on evaluation during a teaching period. If this is the case it may be more appropriate for the therapist to think back over the session when it is complete. It is helpful to consider such issues as how successful the session was in relation to what had been planned, and what might be retained or changed if it were to be repeated. If the teaching session was part of a series, then it is important to consider what should be done the next time. This activity of self-criticism is not always easy since the natural tendency, often born of a lack of confidence, is to promote whatever one is doing (Pring, 1978). This can be overcome, however, by acknowledging to oneself that teaching does not always go to plan, and the important thing is to identify why this should be so.

This informal and continuous approach to evaluation is likely to concern all therapists who undertake a period of teaching, but it is limited in its application since the results may not be sufficiently reliable. It is therefore important to include some formal evaluation, especially if the teaching is extended or likely to be repeated. Something needs to be produced in writing which can be referred to for the future: a common tool of evaluation is the anonymous questionnaire.

A range of questions can be asked, from those which are broad and open-ended, such as:

- What have you enjoyed most about the course?
- What have you liked least about the course?
- What suggestions do you have for improvement of the course?

to those which are focused and closed. An example of a series of closed questions is shown in figure 15.1 where a five-point scale is used for each of the statements.

	Strongly agree	Agree	Neither agree nor disagree	Disagree	Strongly disagree
The depth of content was about right.	☐	☐	☐	☐	☐
The pace was too fast.	☐	☐	☐	☐	☐
I learned something of value.	☐	☐	☐	☐	☐
I found the lectures difficult to follow.	☐	☐	☐	☐	☐
I found the practical work relevant.	☐	☐	☐	☐	☐
The discussion groups were useful.	☐	☐	☐	☐	☐

Figure 15.1 *Example of a series of closed questions*

Another way of recording responses to closed questions is to ask the learner to rank statements by circling the appropriate number, from 1 to 5, where 1 could represent the lowest response and 5 the highest. An example might be:

| supervision was | 1 | 2 | 3 | 4 | 5 | supervision was |
| inadequate | | | | | | adequate |

| treated like a | 1 | 2 | 3 | 4 | 5 | accepted as an |
| 'student' | | | | | | adult learner |

| no time for | 1 | 2 | 3 | 4 | 5 | time available |
| discussion | | | | | | for discussion |

| questions | 1 | 2 | 3 | 4 | 5 | questions |
| discouraged | | | | | | encouraged |

It is useful to include an open-ended question requesting further comment. This will allow the learner to identify aspects of the learning experience which may not have been included on the questionnaire. One of the weaknesses of closed questions is the assumption that all answers are accommodated, but this is rarely the case (Cohen and Manion, 1989). It is, however, much quicker to analyse responses from closed questions and to get an overall 'feel' of what has gone well and what improvements need to be made.

It may be useful to ask learners to evaluate the learning experience by means of small-group discussion. This could be done at the end of a period of clinical or fieldwork practice, where both positive and negative aspects could be identified, and suggestions for improvement made. This not only gives useful feedback to the therapist but can serve to help learners appreciate how much they have achieved.

Higgs (1993) highlights the importance of evaluating both process and product dimensions of a clinical educational programme. Process evaluation is concerned with how the practice experience has been implemented: questions could be asked, for example, about initial orientation, level of supervision, and degree of responsibility given. Product evaluation is concerned with what the learners have achieved: questions could be asked about unexpected results, whether expectations have been met, and if the experience is viewed as worthwhile. A similar approach could be used following a range of learning opportunities implemented by the therapist, such as clinic and theatre visits, or spending time with another professional. It is important to identify how effective such activities are perceived to be by the learners.

Although evaluation during and after the period of teaching is likely to be a prime concern of therapists, if a series of teaching sessions is being planned, the therapist could invite critical comment from a more experienced colleague at the planning stage. Ideas could be offered regarding the relevance of the subject matter as well as the methods of teaching to be used.

Other evaluation methods include the inspection of examination results, the use of written reports, and the identification of research or scholarly activity. These are discussed in the next section.

Who should be involved in the evaluation process?

It is clear from what has been said so far that therapists should evaluate their own teaching, and that learners should be asked for their opinions. Another source of information comes from colleagues who may have assisted in some way. If therapists have been asked to teach some sessions which are part of a larger teaching programme, such as an undergraduate course, then the subject tutor requesting the therapist's input may accompany the learners and observe the sessions with them. When each session is complete the therapist could ask the subject tutor for feedback, particularly relating to the relevance of the content and how it fitted in with the overall teaching programme.

When considering a full undergraduate or postgraduate course, evaluation is also gained by scrutiny of the examination results, noting which questions were answered, which were avoided, and whether or not marks for individual questions were high, low or more evenly spread. Such an analysis can indicate how well an area was learned, where confusion occurred and, to some extent, how well the teacher performed (Cox and Ewan, 1988). It is not unknown, however, for learners to compensate for poor teaching in a subject area, by taking greater responsibility themselves and spending more time in private study (Bligh et al., 1981).

Another source of information is the external examiner. Educational establishments, as part of quality assurance, are obliged to make their courses, including assessment procedures, open to external scrutiny; external examiners are appointed to fulfil this requirement. Their role is to ensure that the learner is justly treated and that the standard of the course is maintained. They monitor the quality of courses in a variety of ways including assessing samples of examination scripts and other course work, examining results across the whole range of assessment procedures, observing practical and practice assessments and talking to learners and teachers. Comments from the external examiners, together with their written reports, provide important feedback to the course team, which is used for evaluation purposes. Therapists may need to meet external examiners, particularly in association with clinical teaching and practice assessments.

Identification of the quality and quantity of articles published and presentations made by individual members of the teaching staff and indications of continuing staff development through attendance at courses or in-service training are also acknowledged evaluation activities. It is less likely, however, that therapists would be part of such evaluation, although they could be asked to submit their curriculum vitae for inspection.

Another useful evaluation activity is for learners to reflect on their own learning for the purpose of self-improvement, as distinct from giving feedback to the therapist about the teaching experience. Davie highlights this aspect, identifying the following functions:

> Firstly, through reflective activities one comes to know what one knows; secondly, one comes to understand the meaning and value of what one knows; and finally, one communicates this new learning to others. (1987: 207)

Implicit in this statement is the recognition that learners should be encouraged to take responsibility for their own learning.

Conclusion

It is clear that evaluation is an essential activity for quality assurance: Cross (1992) emphasizes that it should be collaborative and ongoing. Direct observation and interpretation of discussion is open to bias but, on the other hand, scrutiny of results alone does not indicate the constraints that may have been operating during the teaching and learning process. It is, therefore, unwise to rely excessively on any one method, but rather a range of evaluation activities and techniques should be undertaken, recognizing the strengths and limitations of each.

Part Five

Conferences

16

Organizing Conferences and Presenting Conference Papers

When therapists have gained experience in the teaching role, they may decide to organize a conference, either small or large, for the benefit of the learners they wish to assist. For the purpose of this chapter the term 'conference' will mean anything from an invitation to a guest speaker to address and answer questions from departmental colleagues, to a full-scale convention with six or more speakers, and where interested persons are invited to attend.

Planning a conference

The budget and practical arrangements

A vital thing to think about when planning a conference is the budget, for without a budget little can take place. Even for an evening meeting with one guest speaker who is happy to talk without a fee, the price of the coffee and biscuits must come from somewhere. With a larger event a much bigger budget will, of course, need to be procured and managed. It is possible that the department or institution where the therapist works will have a training budget to cover all or some of the costs, alternatively it may be necessary to ask the conference delegates to pay for their attendance. In either event, if the organizer is in receipt of money to arrange the conference, a very clear record must be kept stating how it has been used.

All money paid out should be receipted and all receipts should be kept.

It is helpful if the organizer has some idea of the number of delegates likely to attend as this will have both budgetary and practical implications. Once this is established careful organization and allocation of space becomes possible. The organizer must have a realistic view of how much time is needed for any given activity. It is no good telling eighty people they have fifteen minutes for coffee if only one person is serving!

If the conference is a large event then it is essential for the organizer to enlist the help of other people and even other agencies. The organizer may, for example, need to communicate with catering, administrative and caretaking staff, as well as those in the media resources department. All of this requires considerable communication and organizational skills.

The speakers

Conference organizers will get the most out of speakers if they are clearly briefed. Every speaker will need some information about the delegates so that the knowledge they impart can be tailored accordingly. Speakers will also need as much knowledge about the whole event as possible; it is useful if they know the order in which the presentations will be given, and whether they will be required to answer questions or take part in discussion. Knowledge of the entire event is useful as it shows the context in which the contributions of individual speakers will be set. Many speakers are happy to be briefed in detail; they often need to select material from a vast field of expertise so it is helpful to know what the conference delegates are particularly keen to hear. A clear brief enables speakers to satisfy the needs of the delegates, and may also help to make the speakers feel more confident when delivering their papers.

Choosing speakers can be a daunting task. Some people who organize conferences regularly make a rule that speakers are recommended by the organizing team or by another person whose opinion is valued. It should be remembered that top academics and writers do not necessarily make the finest speakers. The best conference organizers arrange both speakers and delegates with an awareness of the ways they will complement each other; delegates from many disparate areas of expertise may make it difficult for speakers to impart knowledge successfully. It is also helpful if the speakers complement each other. This does not mean that they have to agree but rather that their contributions are logically linked. Intellectual bridges need to be built between presentations, even if they are diametrically opposed, otherwise the delegates may become confused.

Speakers should be asked what equipment they need and what sort of room they would like. It is useful for them to know what teaching methods other speakers intend to use so that a variety of presentations can be planned. This will help to keep the conference delegates interested and alert. The speakers should be given very clear notification of the time and place of the conference and instructions on how to get to it by public transport and car. Information on parking facilities will also be needed.

Speakers may be engaged well in advance. This is particularly so with large conferences which can take months to organize. In this situation it is wise to keep in touch with the speakers during the intervening period. The first correspondence may, for example, confirm the engagement, the second may give information and ask for the speaker's requirements, and the third, which should be sent a few days prior to the conference, should be a simple reminder of time and place. This final correspondence is also a useful way of dealing with last minute problems and requests.

The delegates

All of those attending the conference should be advised well in advance of the time and place and what, if anything, they need to bring. Delegates also need information regarding the venue, public transport and where to park their cars.

As well as giving the delegates information, the organizer requires information from them too: if lunch is being provided it is essential to know about dietary requirements; if some delegates are wheelchair users or have mobility problems then access must be arranged. A blind delegate may need braille copies of handouts, and a deaf delegate may need an interpreter. The meeting of these requests will produce insurmountable problems if no one has thought about them until the person in the wheelchair is waiting at the bottom of a flight of steps, or the vegetarian can find no meatless dish. The accommodation of all these requirements must be worked out well in advance.

If the plan for the conference is to give delegates choice over the sessions they attend, then those choices can be made before the conference starts. The organizer will then know that speaker A needs a lecture theatre, whereas speaker B, who has just a dozen delegates, needs a small room where informal teaching can take place. In some instances the organizer may find it appropriate to allocate delegates to particular speakers and workshops so that a wide range of expertise and experience may be brought to bear upon a particular topic, or so that workshops are of an appropriate size.

It is clear that the collecting of information from delegates, and the dissemination of information to them before the conference starts, is a prime function of the organizer. The better this can be done the more smoothly the conference will run. Figure 16.1 summarizes the organizer's role in this regard.

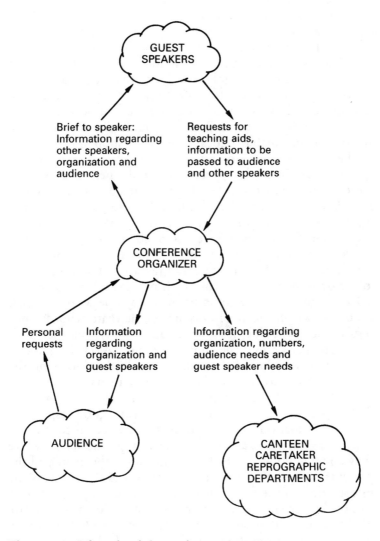

Figure 16.1 *The role of the conference organizer*

Organization on the day

It is a good strategy to begin the conference with time for coffee and general orientation, in which people can relax and introduce themselves; this is important as they may have travelled a long way. Delegates are usually required to register on arrival. The organizer must ensure that they are greeted and that badges and other information are distributed. The conference programme might indicate that registration and coffee will commence at 9.30 a.m, with the conference starting at 10.00 a.m. Sufficient people should be available to show the delegates round. The day should not be marred by anxious people unable to locate their workshop or the library.

There are various domestic arrangements of which delegates should be made aware: where and when lunch will be served, where lunch can be obtained outside the conference centre, where a public telephone is situated and where the toilets are. It is useful to give this information early in the proceedings. Care should be taken not to forget the guest speakers who may arrive throughout the day. Someone should be available to make sure they are not waiting in the lobby or wandering corridors with no idea where to go.

Contingency plans should be made to cope with the small problems which inevitably occur: the delegate who did not return the form but has turned up anyway, another who received a pack about the conference but has left it at home, the speaker who arrives late, and the bulb that blows on the overhead projector just as the first session gets started.

At the end of the conference it is a good idea to ask the delegates to evaluate it. It is possible to get a good response if time for evaluation is built into the conference schedule. It is usual to ask the delegates to fill in a short questionnaire where they comment on a range of issues including the quality of the presentations, the comfort of the venue and the value of the information to their particular situation. Some people prefer to slot this activity in just before the last session as people are likely to rush off as soon as the conference ends. Devising a good evaluation questionnaire is a task which requires considerable time and thought. (For a full discussion of evaluation, the reader is referred to chapter 15.)

Presenting a conference paper

Presenting a conference paper is, in many ways, similar to delivering a lecture. The two activities do, however, differ in certain respects. Conference delegates are likely to possess widely differing areas of expertise and represent a wide range of institutions and work specialities from a large geographical area. They are unlikely to be familiar with the speaker's style of presentation and may bring to the conference a wider variety of expectation, knowledge and understanding than would be expected of learners attending the average lecture.

The presentation of a conference paper is a more formal activity than the delivery of a lecture 'in house' and there may be a sense in which the person who delivers it is a representative of an institution or department. The delivery of the paper, as well as its content, may, therefore, be under scrutiny. Newble and Cannon describe the activity of presenting a conference paper as 'a pressure situation especially for the young and inexperienced hoping to make a good impression on peers and superiors. However it is also a situation which is amenable to resolution by careful planning and technique' (1989: 24).

It is likely that this disparate group of people will not meet again to listen to the same speaker so the limited time allocated must be meticulously planned. This is not so pressing with a lecture where, if it becomes apparent that insufficient time is available, it is often possible to arrange another session. (The reader is strongly advised to read this section in conjunction with chapter 6 on the lecture where many more tips are given.)

Presenting a conference poster

A popular way of displaying research findings at conferences is to design a poster, where the essential points of the research are displayed on a board attached to the wall. It enables interested people to look at the presentation in their own time and to talk to presenters on a one-to-one basis. The size of the poster and details of presentation, for example the size of lettering, are usually stipulated by the conference organizers.

Space is obviously at a premium when designing a poster. What is displayed will depend on the particular research topic, but it will usually include the title of the project, the main reason for carrying it out, a brief description of the methods used, the major results, and the conclusions and recommendations. It must look striking and interesting and be easy to read. The lettering should be more than 5 mm in height, and the text should be broken up with diagrams, photographs, graphs and pictures as appropriate. The use of colour may serve to enliven the poster. Desk-top publishing software can be invaluable when constructing the poster, as can the help and advice of a graphic artist. Some poster displays also make use of other exhibits such as short audio or video recordings, or an explanatory model. A handout and a list of references can also be provided.

Conclusion

Organizing conferences and delivering conference papers is not for the faint hearted; both activities can, however, be achieved by meticulous planning and close attention to the needs of the conference delegates and speakers. The mark of a good conference is when people are able to stimulate each other and broaden each other's horizons. This often has as much to do with the social atmosphere and the exchange of ideas over coffee and lunch than the content and quality of the formal presentations.

References

Adams J.A. (1987) Historical review and appraisal of research on the learning, retention, and transfer of human motor skills. *Psychological Bulletin* 101, 1, 41–47

Adler R.B. and Rodman G. (1991) *Understanding Human Communication*, 4th edn, London, Holt, Rinehart and Winston

Annett J. (1989) Training skilled performance. In Colley A.N. and Beech J.R. (eds) *Acquisition and Performance of Cognitive Skills*, Chichester, John Wiley & Sons

Argyle M., Furnham A. and Graham J.A. (1982) *Social Situations*, Cambridge, Cambridge University Press

Ashcroft K., Gibbs G. and Jaques D. et al. (1990) Using audio-visual aids creatively. Birmingham, Standing Conference on Educational Development, Paper 57, July

Beard R. (1976) *Teaching and Learning in Higher Education*, 3rd edn, Harmondsworth, Penguin Books

Beard R. and Hartley J. (1984) *Teaching and Learning in Higher Education*, 4th edn, London, Paul Chapman Publishing Ltd

Bligh D.A. (1971) What's the Use of Lectures? Harmondsworth, Penguin Books

Bligh D.A. (1980) Methods and Techniques in Post-Secondary Education. *Educational Studies*, 31, Paris, UNESCO

Bligh D., Jaques D. and Warren Piper D. (1981) *Seven Decisions When Teaching Students*, Exeter, Exeter University Teaching Services

Bond D. and Walker D. (1990) Making the most of experience. *Studies in Continuing Education*. 12, 2, 61–80

Brown R. (1988) *Group Processes*, Oxford, Blackwell

Brown S. and Atkins M. (1988) *Effective Teaching in Higher Education*, London, Methuen

Brown S. and Dove P. (1991) Opening mouths to change feet: some views of self and peer assessment. In Brown S. and Dove P. (eds)

Self and peer assessment, Birmingham, Standing Conference on Educational Development, Paper 63, January

Child D. (1986) *Psychology and the Teacher*, London, Cassell

Cohen L. and Manion L. (1989) *Research Methods in Education*, 3rd edn, London, Routledge

Colley A.N. (1989) Learning motor skills: integrating cognition and action. In Colley A.N. and Beech J.R. (eds) *Acquisition and Performance of Cognitive Skills*, Chichester, John Wiley & Sons

Colley A.N. and Beech J.R. (1989) (eds), *Acquisition and Performance of Cognitive Skills*, Chichester, John Wiley & Sons

Cowan J. (1991) Reflections on self assessment. In Brown S. and Dove P. (eds) *Self and peer assessment*, Birmingham, Standing Conference on Educational Development, Paper 63, January

Cox K.R. and Ewan C.E. (eds) (1988) *The Medical Teacher*, 2nd edn, London, Churchill Livingstone

Cross V. (1992) Clinicians' needs in clinical education: a report on a needs analysis workshop. *Physiotherapy*, 78, 10, 758–761

Cull P. (1986) Using audio and visual aids. *Physiotherapy*, 72, 11, 539–542

Curzon L.B. (1990) *Teaching in Further Education: An Outline of Principles and Practice*, 4th edn, London, Cassell

Davie L. (1987) Evolving perspectives of learning, research and programme evaluation. In Boud D. and Griffiths V. (eds), *Appreciating Adults Learning: From the Learner's Perspective*, London, Kogan Page

Dickson D.A., Maxwell A. and Saunders C. (1991) Using role play with physiotherapy students. *Physiotherapy*, 77, 2, 145–153

Douglas T. (1983) *Groups*, London, Tavistock Publications

Elton L. (1984) Evaluating teaching and assessing teachers in universities. *Assessment and Evaluation in Higher Education*, 9, 2, 97–109

Emery M.J. (1984) Effectiveness of the clinical instructor: students' perspective. *Physical Therapy*, 64, 7, 1079–1082

Ford K. and Jones A. (1987) *Clinical Supervision*, London, Macmillan.

French S. (1992) Simulation exercises in disability awareness training: a critique. *Disability, Handicap and Society*, 7, 3, 257–266

French S. (1993) *Practical Research: A Guide for Therapists*, Oxford, Butterworth–Heinemann

French S. and Sim J. (1993) *Writing: A Guide for Therapists*, Oxford, Butterworth–Heinemann

Gardiner D. (1989) *The Anatomy of Supervision: Developing Learning and Professional Competence for Social Work Students*,

Milton Keynes, The Society for Research into Higher Education and The Open University Press

Gibbs G. (1988) *Learning by Doing: A Guide to Teaching and Learning Methods*, London, Further Education Unit

Gibbs G., Habeshaw S. and Habeshaw T. (1988) *53 Interesting Things to Do in Your Lectures*, 3rd edn, Bristol, Technical and Educational Services

Gibbs G. and Habeshaw T. (1990) An introduction to assessment. Birmingham, Standing Conference on Educational Development, Paper 57, July

Gibby B. (1978b) Curriculum evaluation: with reference to some projects. In Lawton D., Gordon P., Ing M. et al. *Theory and Practice of Curriculum Studies*, London, Routledge and Kegan Paul

Griffiths P. (1987) Creating a learning environment. *Physiotherapy* 73, 7, 335–336

Habeshaw S., Habeshaw T. and Gibbs G. (1988) *53 Interesting Things to Do in Your Seminars and Tutorials*, Bristol, Technical and Educational Services Ltd.

Handal G. and Lauvås P. (1987) *Promoting Reflective Teaching: Supervision in Action*, Milton Keynes, The Society for Research into Higher Education and OU Educational Enterprises Ltd.

Hartley J. (1984) *Developing Instructional Text*, London, Kogan Page

Heron J. (1988) Assessment revisited. In Boud D. (ed.) *Developing Student Autonomy in Learning* 2nd ed, London, Kogan Page

Higgs J. (1984) Quality control in continuing education. *The Australian Journal of Physiotherapy* 30, 5, 139–144

Higgs J. (1992) Managing clinical education: the educator–manager and the self-directed learner. *Physiotherapy* 78, 11, 822–828

Higgs J. (1993) Managing clinical education: the programme. *Physiotherapy* 79, 4, 239–246

Honey P. (1988) You are what you learn. *Nursing Times* 84, 36, 34–36

Honey P. and Mumford A. (1982) *The Manual of Learning Styles*. Cited in Jobling M.H. (1987) Cognitive styles: some implications for teaching and learning physiotherapy, *Physiotherapy* 73, 7, 335–338

Hudson L. (1966) *Contrary Imaginations: A Psychological Study of the English Schoolboy*, London, Methuen

Ilott I. (1990) Facing up to the fear of failure. *Therapy Weekly* 17, 10, 6

Janis L.L. (1972) *Victims of Groupthink*, Boston, Houghton Miffin.

Jaques D. (1991) *Learning in Groups*, 2nd edn, London, Kogan Page

Jarski R.W., Kulig K. and Olson R.E. (1989) Allied health perceptions of effective clinical instruction. *Journal of Allied Health*, Fall, 469–478

Jobling M.H. (1987) Cognitive styles: some implications for teaching and learning. *Physiotherapy*, 73, 7, 335–338

Jones K. (1987) *Simulations: A Handbook For Teachers and Trainers*, 2nd edn, London, Kogan Page

Klein J. (1985) *The Study of Groups*, London, Routledge and Kegan Paul

Kolb D.A. (1984) *Experiential Learning: Experience as the Source of Learning and Development*, New Jersey, Prentice-Hall

Maring J.R. (1990) Effects of mental practice on rate of skill acquisition. *Physical Therapy* 70, 3, 165–172

Marshall and Rowland (1983) *A Guide to Learning Independently*, London, Longman

Maslow A.H. (1943) A theory of human motivation. *Psychological Review* 50, 370–396

Mason S.N. (1984) Developing the teaching role of the ward sister. *Nurse Education Today* 4, 1, 13–16

Messick S. (1978) Personality consistences in cognition and creativity. In Messick S. and Associates *Individuality in Learning*, London, Jossey-Bass Publishers

Munroe H. (1988) Modes of operation in clinical supervision: how clinical supervisors perceive themselves. *British Journal of Occupational Therapy* 51, 10, 338–344

Neville S. and French S. (1991) Clinical education: students' and clinical tutors' views. *Physiotherapy* 77, 5, 351–354

Newble D. and Cannon R. (1983) *A Handbook for Clinical Teachers*, Lancaster, MTP Press (Now Kluwer Aademic Publishers)

Newble D. and Cannon R. (1991) *A Handbook for Teachers in Universities and Colleges: A Guide to Improving Teaching Methods*, revised edn, London, Kogan Page

Partridge C. and Barnitt R. (1986) *Research Guidelines: A Handbook for Therapists*, London, Heinemann

Pask G. (1976) Styles and strategies of learning. *British Journal of Educational Psychology* 46, 12–25

Phillips E.M. and Pugh D.S. (1987) *How to Get a Ph.D*, Milton Keynes, Open University Press

Pring R. (1978) Teacher as researcher. In Lawton D., Gordon P., Ing M. et al., *Theory and Practice of Curriculum Studies*, London, Routledge and Kegan Paul

Reid I. (1984) Teaching physiotherapy: a sociological view. *Bulletin of the Association of Teachers of Physiotherapy* 3, 18–21

Rogers J. (1984) *Adults Learning*, 2nd edn, Milton Keynes, Open University Press

Rogers A. (1986) *Teaching Adults*, Milton Keynes, Open University Press

Rogers J. (1989) *Adults Learning*, 3rd edn, Milton Keynes, Open University Press

Rowntree D. (1979) *Assessing Students: How Shall We Know Them?* London, Harper and Row

Rowntree D. (1990) *Teaching Through Self-Instruction: How to Develop Open Learning Materials*, revised edn, London, Kogan Page

Schön D. A. (1983) *The Reflective Practitioner – How Professionals Think in Action*, London, Temple Smith

Skilbeck M. (1984) *School-Based Curriculum Development*, London, Harper & Row

Stengelhofen J. (1993) *Teaching Students in Clinical Settings*, London, Chapman & Hall

Stevenson O. and Parsloe P. (1993) *Community Care and Empowerment*, London, Joseph Rowntree Foundation

Thomas J. B. (1980) *The Self in Education*, Windsor, NFER Publishing Company

Thomas-Edding D. (1987) *Clinical Problem-Solving in Physiotherapy and Its Implications for Curriculum Development*, cited in Best D. (1988) *Physiotherapy Clinical Supervision: Effectiveness and the Use of Models, The Australian Journal of Physiotherapy* 34, 4, 209–214

Thompson I.E., Melia K.M. and Boyd K.M. (1988) *Nursing Ethics*, 2nd edn, Edinburgh, Churchill Livingstone

Walkin L. (1982) *Instructional Techniques and Practice*, Cheltenham, Stanley Thornes

Warner L. and McNeill E.M. (1988) Mental imagery and its potential for physical therapy. *Physical Therapy* 68, 4, 516–521

Watts N.T. (1990) *Handbook of Clinical Teaching*, Edinburgh, Churchill Livingstone

Weiner D. and Bower B. (1982) *Helping Health Workers Learn*, Palo Alto, USA, The Hesperian Foundations

Windom P.A. (1982) Developing a clinical education program from the clinician's perspective. *Physical Therapy* 62, 11, 1604–1609

Wolf J.F. (1980) Experiential learning in professional education: concepts and tools. *New Directions for Experimental Learning* 8, 17–26

The Yerkes-Dodson Law (1908) cited in Child D. (1986) *Psychology and the Teacher*, London, Holt, Rinehart and Winston

Index